"Our perspective is o
understand the perspect
to stop wasting time and start serving qualified clients. As a
sales manager and student of Deb's, I've experienced the real
results of establishing trust through empathy and service.

John Esh
Owner of Joyland Roofing

This book, like it's author, is grounded in clear instruction of
selling you on your best personal self. To my dearest friend
and walking partner... you had the courage to move through
uncertainty to create a book with purpose: *Sell Like Jesus.*

Donna Dee Davis
Personal Close Friend

The early years of my law firm were stagnant. I was reluctant
to pursue "sales" activities, and those I forced myself to
try did not bear fruit. I met Deb Brown Maher, and after a
thought-provoking discussion about her approach to business
development, hired her as a coach. Over time, Deb introduced
me to the principles she has laid out in *Sell Like Jesus.* As I
applied the lessons to my goals and business development
activities, I began to see a dramatic increase in clients and
revenues. Best of all, after working with Deb for over ten
years, I have discovered that I enjoy the process of building
relationships in the business community that is a foundational
part of *Sell Like Jesus.*

Eric A. Welter
Welter Law Firm, P.C.

Deb Brown Maher is a Christian: to know her, is to know that her faith permeates every aspect of her life. It is not surprising therefore that she would look to Christ to guide her as a sales professional. *Sell Like Jesus* is an answer to everyone who has struggled to keep their faith and their integrity intact in the high risk, high reward sales environment. You can have sales success; you can have grateful and even enthusiastic customers. And most importantly, you can be the person you truly believe you should be! Deb doesn't compromise, and neither should you.

Kevin Phelan
General Manager, Avaya Communications

I started my real estate career with Deb when she was with the Sandler System of Sales in the 1990's. As I review this book, I am struck by Deb's deep understanding of the sales process, and feel great joy in the examples of communication and character set forth by Jesus in relationship to being a conscientious salesperson. I now coach real estate agents and believe that salespeople are generally confused about who they should be and how they can communicate without being adversarial. I would HIGHLY recommend this book to anyone in sales.

Donna Fleetwood
Real Estate Coach and NLP Practitioner

Sales is a noble profession, but only if noble people pursue it. Deb Brown Maher proves that an ethical, relationship-focused and Christlike approach to the sales profession can also be highly strategic and financially successful. Recognizing that sales is the key to how organizations serve customers, employ people and support communities, Deb shows sales professionals how to apply Biblical principles and practices to their work in a way that results in demonstrably better sales performance. For Christians and non-Christians alike, the model presented in Sell Like Jesus is enlightening, educational, and will help you improve your experience of, and success in, the selling profession.

Douglas Wendt
President, Wendt Partners

Deb Brown Maher has written a compelling book that turns the stereotypical sales pitch upside-down, sharing valuable insights for anybody trying to sell anything!

Stephanie Marshall
Missionary serving orphans in Romania

Biblical foundation for sales? Deb has lived it and her clients are prospering from it as they apply the methods she teaches. This book will show you how to get the same results.

Bud Handwerk
Owner of Annamar Associates, Inc.

I met Deb in 2007 when she was teaching a '7 Mountains' class at our church, encouraging businesspeople to be more courageous in living their faith in their place of work. There's something that sets Deb apart. She's a "sales coach." I never knew there was "such a thing" until I met her. Although there are a ton of sales resources out there, Deb takes her real life experiences and wraps them into perfect words that work. *Sell Like Jesus* will make you think of things you never would have thought of and will give you answers you will use for the rest of your life.

Myra Leonard
Inn Keeper, Stone Manse Inn Bed & Breakfast

Sales is often considered a high-pressure field; however, after reading this book, you'll realize that when you sell like Jesus, the pressure is off.

Michael McManus

I'm so excited about the *Sell Like Jesus* book! It's been seriously life-changing for my business and I can't wait to get a copy for my team. I was stuck, not seeing the results I knew others have achieved, feeling so frustrated, and questioning myself and my skills. I love helping people, and this book has given me the opportunity through mindset shifts, practical knowledge, and lots of practical action steps to make what's in my heart a reality! By diligently reading each chapter, doing the exercises and putting Deb's biblical-based advice into action, I now feel empowered to see the change I've been longing for. She's not only an amazing author and communicator, she's an excellent coach. I've enjoyed our one-on-one interactions. She really seeks to learn about your situation as she coaches you. Worth the investment for sure!"

Jenny Jackson
Arbonne Consultant

SELL LIKE JESUS

SELL LIKE JESUS

7 CHARACTERISTICS OF
CHRIST FOR ETHICAL SALES

Deb Brown Maher

To David –
May the words on
these pages be an inspiration
to you. God bless the work
of your hands.

Deb Brown Maher
2020

Deb Brown Maher

Library of Congress Cataloging-in-Publication Data is on file with the publisher.

Deb Brown Maher

Publication Cataloging-in-Publiction Data
Sell Like Jesus: by Deb Brown Maher
122 page cm.

ISBN: 978-1-7340557-0-2 Paperback
           978-1-7340557-2-6 ePub
           978-1-7340557-1-9 Mobi
           978-1-7340557-3-3 Audiobook

Printed in the United States of America

In memory of my dad, Bob Miller,
who believed I could do anything I put my mind to.

To my husband, Charles,
who gives me daily encouragement to be and
do everything for which God made me.

With eternal gratitude to my Heavenly Father,
who equips me with divine inspiration and courage to
sell in a way that makes him proud.

Table of Contents

Foreword

This book may well be one of the most powerful tools you ever come across. The difference Deb Brown Maher's sales strategies have made for me has been nothing less than life changing.

Experts say that the number one reason the top 20% of salespeople stand above the remaining 80% is that they hold themselves to a much higher standard. I firmly believe that when we do pursue a higher standard, prosperity is inevitably the outcome.

In this book, Deb demonstrates precisely how to reach that higher standard, using a systematic step-by-step sales approach that works no matter what you are selling. She guides you in developing the necessary intuition to discern who is—and is not—the right client for your business. This ability is key: knowing when to walk away when the Lord prompts you to do so.

In my rewarding, 10-year professional relationship with Deb, she has helped me navigate my personal relationship with Jesus so that I might live my faith through my business. Deb encouraged me to listen and act on God's call to launch a Christian-premised HR firm designed to help organizations do as I had: to navigate being faithful and true to their values in the way they interact with each other and their customers. Despite starting with nothing—no clients, no web presence, and no selling process—we swiftly grew to a national presence, with clients across the US. This success I attribute to Deb's early encouragement and guidance.

It's your turn. Ask yourself: Now that I possess this pivotal guidance, what will I choose to do with it?

It's in your hands.

Mark A. Griffin
Founder and President, In HIS Name HR

Preface

Salespeople often are expected to do their job well with little or no training. It is not uncommon for a new salesperson to be handed a briefcase full of brochures, pamphlets, and a price list and then be told by their boss, "Presto, you're a salesperson." How ludicrous! That wouldn't happen in any other line of work. Professionals and tradesmen alike get more training than that. Achieving excellence at sales requires the same level of study, discipline, and diligence that is needed for excellence in any other profession or occupation.

In recent years, numerous sales training programs have sprung up to meet the needs that the formal education system has ignored. But there are a couple challenges inherent to any off-the-shelf training program, whether about sales or anything else. Firstly, applying general concepts to specific situations requires a level of interpretation and customization before it can be put into effect. There are many nuances to selling different products and services, tangibles and intangibles, not all of which can be covered practically in a general sales training course. It is difficult for most people to apply new structure to an existing situation without some kind of feedback mechanism where they choose what to do, try implementing it, evaluate the results, make adjustments, and try again until they achieve the desired outcome. The frantic pace of most business environments works against this "trial-error-course-correction-try-again" analysis. In the absence of ongoing reinforcement training or ongoing coaching to perpetuate the feedback process, it is difficult to implement what was learned in a way that brings the desired transformation.

Secondly, behavioral change in itself is difficult. Ingrained habits and preferred ways of doing things will always dominate when someone is under pressure. Instituting new habits takes time, hard work, and unwavering commitment to the necessary change.

The fundamental skill that successful salespeople have in common is effective communication. Jesus, through His conversations with friends and adversaries alike, illustrates how to communicate effectively without compromising what He came to do. Compromise implies concession, meaning that someone gives in (loses) to another's position. Buyers constantly ask salespeople to compromise, testing their resolve, indifferent to the loss they are asking the salesperson to accept. Giving in to such requests usually ends badly for the salesperson, and, although it may not be immediately obvious, it goes poorly for the buyer in the long-run, too. Salespeople who give in essentially allow the buyer to take advantage of them, which often breeds resentment. (It's never good to be resentful toward a buyer.) Standing one's ground defensively as a salesperson usually alienates the buyer, who then walks away. (You can never win a fight with a buyer.) Compromise in sales never brings a successful outcome.

Fortunately, Jesus shows us a different way. He shows us how simultaneously to show respect, build trust, and stand our ground in a way that nurtures relationships and allows them to evolve to their logical outcome. This doesn't mean He always got his way; far from it. What it does mean is that He always stood His ground, while respecting the other person's position, never forcing His way on another. He allowed others to decide for themselves, and He accepted their decisions.

What Jesus did and how He did it transcends time and cultures. In these pages you will learn the 7 characteristics that made Jesus a master communicator. Effective communication skills include: listening to understand the meaning behind someone's statements, asking engaging questions, showing respect, and setting clear, mutually beneficial expectations. Life skills such as these build rapport and trust, which in turn develop positive, meaningful, long-term relationships. Developing and employing these skills will improve the quality of all your relationships, personal and professional.

Jesus spent more time communicating in His marketplace than anywhere else. This book will show you how to apply these same characteristics in your marketplace today.

You may be thinking, "Sales and Jesus in the same phrase. Isn't that a contradiction?" On the surface, perhaps. Let's be honest: most people, upon hearing the word "sales," immediately think of someone less than honorable. A lower-life-form that manipulates, lies, and pressures people to do what they don't want to do—all for their own personal gain. Yuck! Disgusting! Don't want to be one of them! This negative stereotype has established a pervasive bad impression that causes most people to shy away from sales as a profession. Can you blame them? How loathed is the sales profession, really? Just ask a thousand children what they want to be when they grow up, and see how many say "salesperson"! The name "Jesus" is another word that evokes a variety of reactions, depending on one's experience. No matter what you believe, His life example and teachings undeniably have influenced society. Even timekeeping is divided according to before (BC) and after (AD) his birth. Now that's impact! There must be something to it.

There are universal truths inherent in Jesus' approach to relationships, as recorded in the Bible, which, when you understand them and put them into action, will change the way you relate to prospects and customers, dramatically improving your sales results. These principles will enable you to transform the sales relationship from adversarial to cooperative, from "convincing someone to buy" to "inviting people to decide for themselves."

The benefits of this approach will be evident not just in bottom-line profits, but also in less quantifiable ways: more highly-motivated salespeople, more productive sales teams, repeat customers, and more word-of-mouth referrals. But the benefits don't stop there. Applying these concepts to all your conversations in every relationship will reap you the rewards of understanding and being understood that bring a level of joy and fulfillment to life unlike anything you've ever known before.

Society would have us believe that good salespeople are born, not made. I disagree. Once you understand the anatomy and psychology of effective communication—what, how, and why— not only will you get better results yourself, but you'll also be able to teach what you've learned to those around you so they get better results too.

This book will expose some long-accepted, but outdated assumptions about how to sell, but, more importantly, introduce a new, flexible, effective sales strategy that can be used by anyone, in any business, in any industry.

It is my desire that the concepts and strategies detailed here will give you new perspectives, new ideas, validation, confirmation, affirmation, and that this book, where needed, will challenge you constructively in ways that will help you communicate more effectively in all of life's circumstances.

Dear Reader,

Thank you for taking the time to investigate what this book is about. My decision to write *Sell Like Jesus* was prompted by talking to countless small business owners, solo-entrepreneurs and freelancers who struggle with the inevitable need to "sell" the product or service they are passionate about. Experience has programmed us to view sales as something "ugly," yet we know it is necessary to start, build, and stay in business. These pages will walk you through a journey to discover some of the preconceived ideas that are holding you back, what you can do to change those perceptions, and then teaches you a way to sell that is comfortable for both you, and those you serve through your business.

Why sell "like Jesus"? Because Jesus is the ultimate model for how to establish, build, and maintain meaningful relationships. When we view sales as a specialized form of relationship building, our perception of what sales really is already starts to shift from something ugly to something desirable.

I am excited for you, and the situation that has brought you to this place at this time, with the desire to learn more about ethical sales. Take your time, enjoy the process as you read and complete the suggested exercises at the end of each chapter. Please consider keeping me apprised of your journey by commenting on the Sell Like Jesus Facebook page, or directly via email at deb@debbrownsales.com.

Here's to your success.

Deb

Chapter 1

What Did Jesus Sell?

Without sales, all businesses fail. Yet, most business owners do not start a business because of a passion to sell something, but rather to make money by getting their product or service into the marketplace. The difference is subtle. The first involves a series of actions that result in a sale, which, for some, conjures up feelings similar to poking a sharp stick in your eye. The second refers to the benefits of having sold: profit, growth, and personal satisfaction, all of which any businessperson would welcome. In spite of U.S. Department of Commerce statistics showing that 80% of businesses will fail by their 5th year, approximately one million new businesses open each year. Being your own boss is increasingly attractive. Sadly, many people discover that the old "build it and they will come" sales model is not enough to succeed in today's competitive environment. The economic realities of this past decade have permanently changed the way many companies do business, and those that have not adapted to changing times have either closed or are still clawing for survival with sales strategies that no longer serve them.

Sales: An Honorable Profession

My own sales story begins in grade school. During the two years I was a Girl Scout, I was top cookie salesperson in my troop. I also loved making and selling those potholders that are made of cloth loops on a little metal loom (amazingly, still available for sale). By age ten I already loved the thrill of the sale. No one taught me; I had no role model or mentor. I just set out on my own and learned as I went. I didn't know enough to take rejection personally. Instead, I plowed on until my inventory of multi-colored designs was gone, and then started production all over again.

Fast forward to my 20s. As a proud recipient of a Bachelor of Arts degree in Latin American Studies, I was qualified to do... you guessed it, not much. So, I sort of backed into my first job: selling. I quickly realized that, somewhere between age ten and twenty, something horrible had happened. Somehow, I had picked up the nagging, self-conscious feeling of not wanting to be perceived as a "salesperson." I heard "no" much more often than "yes," and began taking "no" personally. The stereotype of the pushy salesman, ingrained in my mindset through personal experience, caused me to be conflicted: I still loved the thrill of the "sale" but hated prospects beating me up on price and treating me as if I were sub-human. One day, I decided I had had enough. I was determined to find a better way to sell, a way that would allow me to look myself in the mirror every morning and feel like I was doing good and helping people by selling them what they needed. It was also important to me not to compromise on price, because I couldn't remain employed without generating a profit for the company. That meant I needed a way to not give in to the pressure to please others by dropping my price. The search was on and what you have here, in this book, is the result. It's what I learned that enabled me to become a top producer at one company, and the VP of sales at a startup that later was bought out by a billion-dollar multinational giant.

I am convinced that traditional sales methods are in desperate need of an "upgrade," AND that it doesn't have to take you 20 years to learn how to be wildly successful at sales.

The more I've learned, the more I've seen the need to "simplify" and "demystify" the various facets of sales. I am driven to help others shorten their learning curve by sharing the secrets to sales success that I have discovered so that they can reap the rewards that come with growing their business faster! Why would I want to do that? Because one of the key things I've learned from sales is that the best way to get my own needs met in life is to give to others first. I trust that when I bring value to another, they will repay me by embracing, living, and passing on the information they learn. And when you live out what you've learned, your friends and colleagues will take notice and want what you have. That means more referrals, which are the best kind of sales leads.

Let's be clear: this book won't change your life unless you truly want to change. I can point the way, provide a path, but you have to decide to walk it. Change is a must, and change hurts. No sugar-coating here. The old expression, "No pain, no gain," is all too true. The key is to recognize where you are, identify where you want to be, and then take calculated risks to do things differently, not just for the sake of "different," but because you believe you'll get better results.

The key to change is to take action; do something different! Head knowledge is just that: it stays in your head. Understanding comes through actions that apply what you know. Wisdom is the result of knowledge plus understanding accumulated through multiple experiences. For this reason, I conclude each chapter with recommended action steps that will help you accelerate your learning by implementing quickly, in a controlled way. Remember, changing behavior is a process; a journey, not an event. For those of you who will read this book all the way through, skipping the exercises, I strongly urge you to consider a second reading of the book to complete the exercises. Just remember, until your actions change, your circumstances won't change either.

You may be wondering exactly what life looks like from the other side of this journey. Over the years, my clients have shared things like:

"Sales used to be drudgery. Now it is fun!"

"Having a plan has made all the difference in my sales results."

"Our team used to be on the bottom, but now we hit #1 regularly."

"I no longer have to guess why someone does or does not do business with me. I know exactly why, and that helps me keep my attitude straight."

"I learned that when the phone stops ringing there are actions I can take to go find the business."

"I used to feel like sales was a 'numbers game,' and there was nothing I could control except doing 'more activity.' I was already working as hard as I could. Now I know that I have control over the way my sales conversations unfold. It is more about the quality of the interaction."

"I learned that sometimes it is best not to do business together, and that's okay! I no longer take on clients that look like 'trouble.'"

I invite you to take this journey of self-discovery and change with me. Are you ready to get started? Here we go!

One could argue quite successfully that Jesus didn't "sell" anything; rather, He "gave it all." Yet, He managed to get buy-ins from enough people to completely turn the course of world events. By communicating a new perspective on a set of long-held and well-established beliefs, Jesus became the catalyst for a new way of living. When He invited others to explore that new perspective, many accepted His invitation.

The Problem with "Sales"

Let's be real: if we were playing the TV game-show *Password*,[1] and the word I was trying to have you guess was "salesperson," Jesus is the last clue you'd expect. "Used car," "slick," or "slime-ball" would be more likely to produce the right answer. Why is that? It's simple; we've all had a bad experience with a "salesperson" who manipulated us, lied to us, or played on our fears for their own personal gain. It only takes one negative interaction with one of "those" offensive salespeople to color our perception of every other salesperson we meet from then on. This negative stereotype, and not wanting to be associated with "one of them," causes many accomplished, kind, smart, capable people to struggle when they find themselves having to operate in a sales role.

The very definition of sales—the fair exchange of goods or services in return for agreed upon compensation—implies a win for both parties. Each gives and receives according to mutual agreement.

What did Jesus sell? An eternal relationship with the triune God: Father, Son, and Holy Spirit. That relationship with God also serves as the model for all relationships we have with one another. What was the currency Jesus accepted? Giving up of self: self-reliance, self-protection, self-promotion, self-sufficiency, and selfish desires. What do we get in return? An eternal, intimate relationship with the Creator of the universe, to know Him in a way that goes far beyond what words can describe. Through that relationship with God, we are also

---

[1] Password was a television game show popular in the United States in the 1960s. There were two teams, each consisting of a famous celebrity and a contestant. The show host revealed a secret word, the Password, to one member of each team, and to the television audience. The team members with the Password had to get their partners to guess it correctly by feeding them one-word clues. The first pair to guess the Password correctly received a point. https://en.wikipedia.org/wiki/Password_%28game_show%29

positioned to influence others in a way that is impossible to achieve otherwise. Using an analogy to illustrate the difference, when we join with Christ, our efforts are transformed from shades of gray to brilliant technicolor.

It is from the position of resting in our relationship with Him that we can become more like Him in all our interactions with people, both in our personal lives and at work. We're going to explore seven characteristics of how Jesus approached people that helped Him bring transformational power to people and situations. We'll specifically look at applying those characteristics in sales.

If you subscribe to Judeo-Christian values, your moral compass can wreak havoc on your ability to sell as you try to maintain your ethical values in the business world. Since the 1990s, I've worked with hundreds of business owners and sales professionals who share these and other common themes of inner conflict:

- Finding the balance between giving and receiving. How do you overcome the fear of setting a fair profit margin and not giving in just because someone asks for a lower price?
- Being honest in all your dealings even if it means telling someone you can't profitably do what they are asking for.
- Not compromising your values to win a customer when they ask you to do something that may be "legal" but goes against your sense of right and wrong.

Staying true to yourself, your values, and your God when faced with real pressures to pay the bills and feed your family can cause the kind of emotional turmoil that keeps people awake at night. How do you cope? The automatic, biological response to that kind of pressure is "fight" or "flight." In tough sales situations, a fight response may look like agreeing to lower your price and then getting angry at the client for "making you" do it. A flight response could manifest as not asking for the business, or not following through on opportunities because you convince yourself that doing so would bother the prospect and cause you to lose the sale. Although fight and flight have merit when our lives are truly being threatened, if allowed to operate unchecked in a sales relationship (or any relationship for that matter), they undermine the possibility for mutually beneficial outcomes.

If this sounds familiar, you are in good company. Thousands of business owners and professionals start businesses every year because of a passion for their craft, NOT because they wanted to "sell" their product or service. You believe that people will buy from you, or you never would have opened your business in the first place. But having to actually market and actively sell challenges some of the most brilliant people I have met. The inability to sell effectively puts 80% of businesses out of business before the 5-year mark.

The good news is that there is another way, where you can take the lead to orchestrate conversations that benefit everyone. The author of that approach is Jesus, and the seven characteristics He displayed that foster ethical sales are: character, connection, clarity, comprehension, certainty, choice, and commitment. We'll explore each one in depth in the chapters to follow.

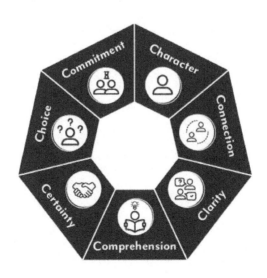

⧉⇥ Key Points to Remember:

1. Sales is not a "dirty word." It is an honorable profession.
2. It is possible to be wildly successful at sales and simultaneously stay true to ethical standards.
3. Fight or flight responses have no place in a sales conversation.
4. You can learn to orchestrate mutually beneficial sales conversations by implementing relationship-building strategies modeled by Jesus Christ.

⟨⟩ Action Steps:

1. If you have a love-hate relationship with sales, take some time to make two lists: what you love, and what you hate. Save these lists and revisit them as you work your way through this book. Write down additional insights as they occur.
2. What exactly are you hoping to learn as you read the rest of this book? Feel free to share your answers with me at deb@debbrownsales.com.
3. Visit www.debbrownsales.com/sljworkbook to get a free downloadable Sell Like Jesus workbook.

Chapter 2

Characteristic #1: Character— Identity and Purpose

All children show what they're really like by how they act. You can discern their character, whether they are pure or perverse.
(Proverbs 20:11)

Character emerges as we express ourselves in relationship with others, through the choices we make on how we interact in different situations. The sales relationship is often stereotyped as adversarial, where the seller wants to take the buyer's money, and the buyer wants to keep it. In the absence of a transformational force, this set of opposing desires drives the behavior of both buyer and seller, which perpetuates the stereotype. Both parties'

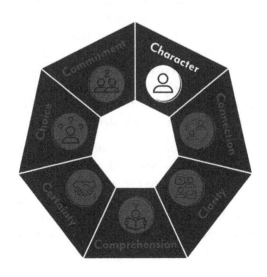

actions are reduced to survival tactics, despite whatever good intentions either side may have had to begin with.

You may have heard it said that to make it in sales you need to have "rhino-skin," a tough hide, in order to take all the abuse that buyers dish out. I agree you have to be strong, but not in that self-protective way. Real strength comes from knowing who you are, being who you are, and acting in ways that show you are clear about what you are trying to accomplish. Operate as a person of integrity, doing what you say you'll do, when you say you'll do it. Let your actions witness to your character and affirm your intentions. A firm identity is the root of real strength, courage, security, and resilience. And if you've ever done sales, you know you need it!

Seeking affirmation for who you are from others, especially prospects, always opens the door to disappointment. John Wooden said, "Be more concerned with your character than your reputation, because your character is what you really are, while your reputation is merely what others think you are." A strong sense of character allows you to draw courage from the inside so that you can enter the fray of what begins as the stereotypical sales conversation and take actions that change it, reshape it, and transform it into a positive, effective, and satisfying interaction for both parties. You have a choice. You can be the one who sets the tone by orchestrating the sales conversation to achieve the most beneficial outcome for everyone involved. That takes strong character, a knowledge of self, and comfort with one's own identity.

Jesus brought radical change to the world that has withstood the test of time, and it is His example that we, too, can employ to get lasting results. He transformed society one conversation at a time. By rejecting the traditional adversarial and manipulative sales tactics that are prevalent in sales today, we can also transform the established norms of selling by instituting specific actions to shift the quality of the sales relationships we engage in.

Self-Aware and Mission-Focused

What sustained Jesus so that He could complete His work? First of all, an awareness of who He was—His identity—demonstrated by the consistency of character He displayed in all His conversations. His mission, what He did in relationship with others, was a direct expression of His character and was completely congruent with it. He was sure enough in who He was and what He was doing that He never compromised His standards even when things got hard. When opposition threatened to shut Him down, He remembered His mission and stayed true to Himself, summoning the courage to do what was needed to accomplish His work.

Jesus faced being put to death; whatever we face in the sales arena is minor in comparison. But in the moment, it doesn't feel minor. I'll never forget the time that a gruff, white-haired, successful businessman challenged me skeptically, "Why should I buy from you?" I was so caught off-guard, that my survival, fight-or-flight mechanism kicked into overdrive. Possible answers flooded my brain, and I summarily dismissed each one as quickly as I thought it, knowing that they would all sound defensive at best and "combative" at worst. It felt like a trap and I had no strategy for dealing with it. Even though I was sitting down, my knees knocked together frantically. I froze. (Heavy sigh...)

That experience fueled my determination to find a way to answer similar future challenges from a position of confidence, rather than a posture of defensiveness where I feared I might antagonize or feel the urge to apologize for my position. At the end of this chapter we'll look at the following technique in detail, but the essence of it is to acknowledge and affirm the person's challenge, then ask a question to gain agreement on a dialogue that will help the person answer their own question.

Acknowledge, Affirm, and Shift Direction with a Question

This framework can be used effectively no matter the challenge facing you. But before we look at it in more detail, we first need to address the factors that can keep you from using the framework. Knowledge is power only when we can put that knowledge into action. And fear, in many forms, can trip us up unless we're prepared to press through it.

Actions flow out of belief. Said another way: if I think I can, I can. Likewise, if I think I can't, I can't. Having a strong sense of who you are, respecting yourself for the unique qualities you bring to those around you, is the foundation from which you sell most effectively.

Things that Undermine Self-Confidence and Threaten Self-Control

Operating in the role of salesperson brings inherent triggers that can undermine sales success and tempt us to act in ways that compromise who we are in order to satisfy an immediate emotional need (fight or flight). We must acknowledge and deal with these triggers in order to orchestrate a better outcome. Here are some questions to help raise your level of emotional intelligence and start the process of changing your thoughts and controlling your responses so they line up with and support your mission. These questions address three areas that I see many salespeople and business owners struggle with: identity vs. role, money, and fear of rejection.

Identity versus Role

Does the title on my business card include the word "sales"? If not, why not? Is it fear of rejection, criticism, or feeling discredited?

Don't confuse who you are with what you do for a living. Sales is a role that you play, it isn't your character or your identity. In case you've never realized this, let me say it as clearly as I can: *you have intrinsic value as a human being.* There is no one else on the planet exactly like you; never has been, and never will be. That means you have inherent value that you bring to every relationship that you cultivate. You bring "you"—with all your unique knowledge, perspectives, abilities, and character traits—with you to every role that you play. It is essential to your emotional health to separate who you are as a person from what you do at work, or any other role that you play. Why? Because otherwise, role failures can be misconstrued as personal failures, and it is impossible to continue to perform at your best when you feel like a failure. By separating who you are (your identity) from what you do (roles you play), you can be more objective when you fall short of role expectations, learn from them, and press forward to improve. Remember that you are not a failure. You may have failed at something, but that thing doesn't define who you are as a person.

When it becomes hard to keep selling, whether because you've heard "no" too often, or a deal fell through, or people just seem to be nasty in spite of your best efforts to help them, remember: sales is a role that you play. If you don't like the results you're getting, look objectively at your actions and your knowledge. Assess where you might have a gap, learn something new, try it, evaluate it, and keep on learning and growing until you reach your desired outcomes.

Courage to sell when the going gets tough comes from understanding that what you do isn't who you are. The day I confessed to a gathering of Christian business people that God made me good at sales, and publicly embraced in front of them all that I was a salesperson as a way to honor the gift that God put in me, is the day that I started being successful in my sales consulting business. Before that, I was double-minded; I knew I was designed to make my living at sales—and helping others do the same—but I kept resisting it because of the fear of being judged negatively by others simply because I was in sales. Double-mindedness breeds confusion and undermines success.

In Matthew 5:37 Jesus reminds us that, "A simple "Yes" or "No" will suffice. Anything beyond this springs from a deceiver."

Make a decision to sell—or not to sell, but then do something else that you are passionate about instead. The choice is yours. I could have taken a safer route by returning to a job in the corporate world. But the truth is that I knew God made me to do sales coaching and training in a unique way, and I could only do that by starting my own company. We cripple ourselves when we succumb to thinking that we can get by without fully committing to doing what we are made for. Let your yes be yes, and your no be no. In January 2008, fully committed in heart and mind, I started my sales consulting business. My second year in business tripled my first year's earnings, and my third year tripled my second year's earnings.

What has to change in the way you think about sales to enable you to say, "I'm in sales and I'm proud of it?"

It's important to replace destructive thoughts with a constructive counterpart that will help you move toward your desired outcome. Here is an example: if you feel that sales is adversarial, and now you realize that thought is setting you up to be combative when challenged by a prospect, what is an alternative view that you can adopt, practice, and eventually live by that will change your outcomes? It might be something like this: sales is a puzzle, where both parties have to understand the pieces and see if they fit with each other; or, sales is a dance where both parties have to learn each other's moves to see whether they click or whether it's better to sit the next one out.

Money

Ask yourself, do I feel like I deserve the monetary success that being good at sales can provide?

Everyone has strong feelings about money. No one wants to be poor, or to be seen as greedy. Yet, consider this: poverty and greed are two sides of the same coin that reads, "Money: I can never get enough of it." Your relationship to money underlies every sales conversation you have. Do you approach sales the same way whether you're in debt and pressed to pay bills, or it's mid-month and you've already met your quota and are well on your way to earning a bonus?

First Timothy 6:10 says, "Loving money is the first step toward all kinds of trouble..." To determine your current relationship to money, answer this question: *Do I control my money or does my money control me?* If you answered the former, good for you. If you answered the latter, spend some time looking at your own situation and determine what needs to change. Then put a plan into action that brings you back into control over your finances. This will help alleviate the pressure to "sell at any cost," which can result in negative consequences like:

- Pressing so hard that the buyer says yes to your face, but later cancels the order.
- Lowering your price because you're afraid to lose the sale, and later realizing you're not making any profit, or, worse, you're losing money.
- Taking shortcuts on the solution you provide, hoping no one will notice, but they do, and it causes them to badmouth you and your company to anyone who will listen.

Fear of Rejection

No one likes to be rejected. But remember, like baseball players at bat, successful salespeople only average two or three "hits" out of every ten efforts. Ask yourself: *How do I take it when a prospect tells me "no"? What kinds of things do I hold back from discussing for fear of making someone upset? How do I address objections—or do I ignore them and retreat instead?*

Romans 12:2 says, "Stop imitating the ideals and opinions of the culture around you, but be inwardly transformed by the Holy Spirit through a total reformation of how you think…" In the context of sales, that means stop trying to please everyone around you for fear that they will reject you. Instead, work on learning how you want to be perceived, set your course, and don't waver from it, asking the Holy Spirit to teach you and strengthen your ability to do the hard thing because it is the right thing to do—regardless of what anyone else may think.

This isn't easy to do. It takes diligent, hard work to influence the dynamic of a sales conversation, so you won't do it if you're afraid of losing face, offending someone, or being criticized.

Let's revisit the prospect's challenge mentioned earlier, and apply the Acknowledge, Affirm, Shift Direction With a Question strategy:

Prospect says: "Why should I buy from you?"

Salesperson: "Great question. At this point, I'm not sure that you should, because I really don't know you nor do I understand what you might need. Would you be open to having a conversation so we can learn about each other to see if it makes sense to move forward or not?"

Prospect says: "What makes you better than xyz company?"

Salesperson: "No matter how I answer, it will fall short, because it isn't my definition of "better" that matters here; it's yours. So, may I ask you, what are you hoping that I will be able to help you with?

Prospect says: "That's too expensive."

Salesperson says: "Ah… and that would be compared to what…?"

Prospect says: "Your bid is the highest one we've gotten."

Salesperson says: "Thanks for sharing that with me. We're often the highest bid, yet we have a lot of satisfied customers. Why do you think they were willing to pay more in order to hire us?"

Start using the Acknowledge, Affirm, Shift Direction With a Question strategy whenever you feel challenged, at any time during the sales process, and share your best practices with me at deb@debbrownsales.com. I always love to hear your success stories.

ᴥ Key Points to Remember:

1. Character, the expression of our identity, is where everything it takes to be good at sales starts, because what we believe about ourselves will drive our actions. People can't read your mind or your intentions; they judge you by what you say and do. So, say and do things differently, in a way that demonstrates your good intentions and gets you better results.

2. Remember: if you think you can, you can. If you think you can't, you won't be able to.

3. You can orchestrate sales conversations to be collaborative instead of adversarial by listening, acknowledging, and asking questions.

4. Take a hard look at the things that might be undermining your success, especially how you see yourself, how you view money, and how you interpret the word "no." These three areas can sabotage even the smartest, most capable person on the planet.

⟨⟩ Action Steps:

1. Write down why you want to be a successful salesperson. Take your first answer, and ask yourself "why" again, in relation to what you said. Repeat this process five times, or until you get to the root of what motivates you. The better

you understand your "why," the easier it is to sustain the right behavior during tough times.

2. Consider any negative thoughts, attitudes, or habits you have that interfere with your sales success. Name them, question their usefulness, and decide which ones you need to let go. Fill the void with positive alternative thoughts and actions. Practice saying and doing them until they become a habit. (See Dr. Carolyn Leaf, *Switch on Your Brain* for details on how to permanently change your thoughts.[2])

3. Enlist the help of a friend, colleague, or coach with whom you can share your plan and to whom you can be responsible to report your progress.

---

[2] Dr. Caroline Leaf, Switch On Your Brain: The Key to Peak Happiness, Thinking, and Health. (Grand Rapids: Baker Books, a division of Baker Publishing Group, 2013).

Chapter 3

Characteristic #2: Connection— Target Audience and Approach

Now, remember, it is I who sends you out, even though you feel vulnerable as lambs going into a pack of wolves. So be shrewd as snakes yet as harmless as doves. (Matthew 10:16)

Knowing who you want to reach and how you structure your approach to reach them is the foundation for connecting with prospects in a meaningful way. Living out of the firm foundation of an unwavering character, and knowing what He wanted to accomplish, Jesus entered the marketplace at age thirty with a clear and consistent message. He came to restore mankind's ability to have an ongoing, eternal relationship with God that

was lost as a consequence of Adam and Eve's choice to become self-reliant, thereby rejecting God.[3]

In essence, Jesus "sold" the ability for every person to have an intimate relationship with God the Father, the Creator of the Universe. Further, that relationship could start immediately here on earth, upon acceptance of the terms of the contract: admit that you've sinned; repent and turn away from sinful habits; accept and declare Jesus as Lord and spend the rest of your life on earth pursuing a deeper relationship with Him. The bonus: your relationship with God will never end, even after your physical body dies.

Jesus' method to restore us to God was to model the relationship that He promised—by building relationships to do it! He was a living example of how we, too, can build relationships to find those who want what we offer. We've all met people who are quick to engage in a superficial relationship but who don't follow through to build depth in that relationship over time. These

---

[3] The first man, Adam, and his wife, Eve, were created by God to have an intimate, eternal relationship with Him. Instead of trusting God for everything, however, they listened to the serpent's lie that eating the fruit of the forbidden tree would make them like God, having the knowledge of good and evil. When they dared to think that they themselves could be equal to God, and therefore self-reliant, they rejected God's complete and perfect provision and subjected themselves to the same fate as Satan, a fallen archangel who made himself the enemy of God by trying to claim equality with God. God is a righteous judge, and His righteousness demands payment for rebellion. Satan's rebellion was punished by being cast out of God's presence, forever separated from God and His heavenly dwelling place, eternally damned to an existence in hell.

God is bound by His own irrevocable laws to punish rebellion. If He banished Satan from heaven and judged him to eternal life in hell for his rebellion, then man had to come under the same punishment—or else God would not be just. So, because of Adam and Eve's rebellion, man was cast out of God's presence, out of the Garden of Eden, and experienced separation from God from that day forward. Their act of rebellion determined that all mankind would be born into the state of separation from God. Man would have to suffer the same fate of eternal separation from God that Satan incurred, except for the life, sacrificial death, and resurrection of Jesus, the Son of God, who personally took the punishment for man's sin and provided a path to restored relationship with God the Father.

individuals sometimes achieve high levels of success, but they tend to fall just as quickly, and when they do, they fall alone, because they haven't cultivated lasting connections with others.

Target Audience

Jesus wasn't trying to reach everyone during the three years He took his offering public. His target audience was narrow and specific, as seen here in the instructions He gave his disciples in Matthew 10:6-7: "…Don't go into any non-Jewish or Samaritan territory. Go instead and find the lost sheep among the people of Israel." In other words, Jesus' target audience was the people of the twelve tribes of Israel, the Jewish nation. On rare occasions when it was recorded that He dialogued with non-Jews, He only did so when they met the qualification of having deep faith in Him as the Messiah. (See, for example, Luke 7:1-10; Matthew 15:22-28; John 4:7-41.) His disciples followed suit, concentrating their efforts on the Jewish people. It wasn't until eight years[4] after His primary audience heard His message, when Peter was sent by the Lord to the house of Cornelius (see Acts chapter 10), that His followers started to expand their reach to people-groups other than the Jews.

Who is in your target audience? Think about who stands to gain the most from engaging with you, and think about your best, favorite, wish-you-had-a-hundred-of-them customer. That group is your sweet-spot in the marketplace. When you focus your offerings and messaging around how you solve the problems that this particular group of people have, you have a highly focused sales approach that will help you both deliver and reap maximum rewards. The reality of sales is that those who are not in your sweet-spot will find you anyway, and some will want to hire you anyway. Just as Jesus "qualified the level of

---

[4] https://www.churchathome.org/day-jesus-died/pdf/Chronology%20V.pdf

faith" in the non-Jews He aided, you can qualify those who are outside your main area of expertise and determine when you'll take them on as a client, and when it's better to help them find someone else who is better suited to meet their need.

Within Jesus' target audience were three types of groups that He interacted with regularly: the Jewish religious leaders, His inner circle of twelve disciples, and the large crowds who came to hear him teach. Developing lasting relationships is the primary skill needed to succeed at sales. Jesus demonstrated this skill with each group using three different but overlapping approaches that fostered dialogue and provided people with the information they needed to make a decision whether or not to buy what He was selling.

The Approach: Build Relationships

Jesus modeled a respect-based relationship by being the first to give respect where respect was due. He was a complex individual who was bringing revolutionary change to a tradition-bound people. He knew that He needed to gain the trust of those who might not see things His way, in order to lay the groundwork for His ministry. As a child of twelve years old, Jesus met with the Jewish teachers and leaders at the temple in Jerusalem.[5] He demonstrated respect by listening to them first, then He asked questions that showed a level of wisdom and understanding that was atypical for anyone, let alone a boy that age. Even before saying anything declarative, Jesus used His listening skills and the nature of His questions to elicit interest and engagement among individuals who were many years older than He, and who had no logical reason to take Him seriously. In short, He showed great respect for them and in so doing, enabled them to become open to offering great respect back.

---

[5] See Luke 2:46-47.

These teachers may not have become close personal friends of His, nonetheless these relationships had a lasting impact because (a) He built a relationship based upon mutual respect and trust, and (b) those teachers and leaders were changed because of the encounter. Even after His departure, He changed their way of thinking forever. Therefore, although the relationships may not have continued, they did result in a long-term impact.

The second kind of lasting relationship is experience-based relationship. Jesus knew that to build a core leadership team (His disciples), He needed to go beyond showing mutual respect and specifically focus on building mutual trust through ongoing interactions and shared experiences. They became His full-time students, first learning what He taught, then doing it and ultimately teaching others as well. They got to experience His teaching, not just listening to it, but also putting it into action. This group received personal instruction and intimate knowledge and insight directly from Jesus that no one else did. They were His "ideal customers," who "bought" the highest priced package—the one that required them to give up everything, even their lives, in order to receive the full measure of what He offered. Throughout His ministry, Jesus' message, His reason for being, revolved around the importance of building lasting relationships—those that stand the test of time, and which create a deep sense of personal commitment on the part of both participants.

The third type of lasting relationship Jesus demonstrated was that of teacher. Many people were curious about His message and came to His "workshops on the hillsides" to learn and grow. In these encounters He raised the awareness of those in attendance, inviting them to enter into a new way of thinking, and to ultimately join the ranks of the apostles if they would so choose. Jesus never compromised His message to appeal to the masses. He delivered the same message that the religious leaders and His close disciples heard, but His delivery method with each group was appropriate to the circumstance. In the case of the large crowds, He presented information in a way that was understandable to an audience that didn't have the schooling that the religious leaders or the disciples had. They were at the "entry-level" of understanding, and needed to learn basics first in order to make a decision to buy in or not. Unlike the disciples, who dropped everything and committed their lives immediately upon hearing Jesus' invitation to follow Him, these people went through a different learning and decision-making process. Jesus frequently taught with stories and analogies that were able to convey difficult and sometimes challenging concepts in ways that plain and ordinary folk could easily grasp and ponder.

Jesus knew that respect and trust were the essential ingredients in building lasting relationships, and that the ability and commitment to creating and sustaining lasting relationships was essential to the life of a leader. Did this mean that Jesus was always successful in maintaining relationships on His terms? Surely not. Some people never trusted Him, or turned their backs on His efforts when challenged to change. Others (like Peter) became fearful and struggled with doubt at many points. Still others turned on Jesus and betrayed Him.

And that brings us to the final ingredient that is essential to building lasting relationships: the willingness to keep building them, even after some have failed and others have turned against you. Despite the actions or failings of others, Jesus continued to commit His life to creating lasting relationships: with leaders and servants, individuals and communities. This is exactly what we are called to do as sales professionals today.

How can a Christian business owner or sales professional learn from Jesus' example when it comes to building business relationships? After all, aren't business relationships very different from personal friendships or Christian charity?

Certainly, they are different from one another. However, they all have one thing in common: they are still relationships, regardless of the setting.

Here are four key points on building relationships to consider, strategize, and put into action.

1. *Prospects are everywhere, not just in the obvious places.*

Jesus didn't just look to build relationships where He thought it was most valuable, relevant, or ideal. He built relationships everywhere—and won hearts and minds everywhere as well. While ministry certainly has a broader "target market" than selling a specific product or service, the same idea applies: new opportunities can arise from just about anywhere. Stories abound in the business press about particularly enthusiastic and engaged executives and sales professionals who encountered major business opportunities outside the office: at the soccer field, in a restaurant, on a flight, or in church or civic settings. The key lesson is to *always be open to new introductions and new relationships.* You never know where they might lead.

2. *Establishing trust begins with empathy and engagement.*

Another advantage to being open to new relationships in a wide range of contexts is that it conditions you to develop relationships across a wide range of settings and circumstances, which requires you to become a better listener. Listening and observing are essential to understanding and asking targeted questions. Everybody wants to feel like they are being heard, so listening with the intent to truly understand the other person is instrumental to building trust. Any form of assumption-making cuts off listening and eliminates curiosity to know more or understand at a deeper level. If you think you know something, you won't ask, and that terminates communication. Jesus always asked insightful, diagnostic questions, learned about each person's unique circumstances, avoided passing judgment, and demonstrated empathy and true personal engagement every time, even when those closest to Him pressured Him to ignore the person in His path so they could stick with the schedule.

3. *Examples and stories are essential to the discussion.*

In addition to His unique way of listening, Jesus also demonstrated a unique way of speaking, always presenting stories and examples that made His ideas clear and His concepts memorable. That approach was effective enough to make Jesus' stories last 2,000+ years, and it is equally relevant to your work today. Studies show that when you tell a story to illustrate a business concept or point, you increase the likelihood that it will be remembered by up to three times. Storytelling also creates more intimacy and engagement on the part of the other person in the conversation. We're naturally wired to remember stories rather than just facts, and with the increasing complexity of today's products and services, often loaded with features and benefits that are impossible for anyone to remember, storytelling becomes even more essential.

4. *You must believe in the transformative power of your solution.*

Jesus was absolutely convinced of the value of what He had to offer. He believed to His core that the solution He offered to each individual was the right one, and was unquestionably going to make their lives better. You may intellectually believe that your products and/or services are valuable, but unless you really empathize with your customer and become personally engaged in understanding and responding to their needs, you will not be able to deeply demonstrate a personal belief in support of your solution. That's why it's so important to take the time to create, tailor, and configure solutions for your clients, rather than just selling products or services.

☞ Key Points to Remember:

1. Connecting begins with knowing who can benefit most from what you sell, and how to approach them in a way that increases the likelihood that they will be receptive to what you offer.
2. Relationship building is a long-term endeavor, and requires an investment of time and energy to listen, hear, and respond in ways that deepen the relationship.
3. Some relationships result in a sale more quickly than others; some never result in a sale. That doesn't mean that those relationships aren't valuable and worth cultivating.
4. Everyone leads you to someone; the connection you make with any given person may reap results because of people they know that they will introduce you to.
5. One of the best ways to establish trust is to listen and be inquisitive to learn more about what your prospect is saying.
6. If you don't believe in yourself and what you are selling, no one else will either.

⟨⟩ Action Steps:

1. List three ways that you can open up new and diverse relationships. Think about connecting with people with the motive of being able to serve them somehow.
2. Listen and get curious! Practice listening, not just with your ears, but with your heart, mind, and whole being. Then implement a new level of curiosity that includes asking questions to obtain a deeper understanding of what you've just heard. Try asking not just one follow up question, but follow up the second and third responses with additional, clarifying questions. After the conversation do a "before and after" review of what you learned. How much more do you know about that person now compared to before your conversation? How do you feel toward them, and they

toward you afterward, compared to before? Was it worth the extra time it took in the moment to gain that information?

3. Too many salespeople focus on their product, service, features, and benefits, leaving out the more compelling emotional reason someone buys. For example: if the things your product/service can do are called features (this curling iron heats up in 10 seconds) and the results your product/service provide are called benefits (so I don't have to wait forever to get on with curling my hair), then what is the problem/pain that is eliminated? (I can sleep later because it no longer takes so long to curl my hair in the morning.) Pain is personal, and only the customer can define what is "worth" paying to eliminate. What problems do you, your products, and your services fix for your customers? What pain gets eliminated when they do business with you? List as many pain points as you can possibly think of and how your offering fixes them. Then, as part of your initial conversation, ask your prospects if those things are important to them. When you demonstrate a clear understanding of the pain a prospect is in, they automatically assume that you know how, and are able, to fix it. This approach will transform the nature of your sales conversations and will demonstrate your trustworthiness.

Chapter 4

Characteristic #3: Clarity— Preparation and Setting Expectations

...Jesus began to proclaim his message with these words: "Keep turning away from your sins and come back to God, for heaven's kingdom realm is now accessible." (Matthew 4:17)

Jesus took great care to make sure His message was easy to understand. In Matthew 4:17 He quickly and clearly communicated three things:

1. *The "product" that was available—the accessibility of heaven's kingdom realm.*
2. *The "cost"—turn away from your sins.*

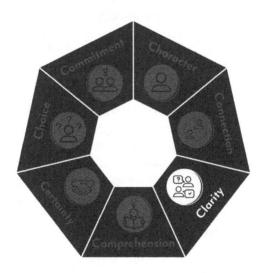

3. *The "merchandise" you would enjoy—a restored relationship with God.*

The content of Jesus' message was unerringly consistent and always centered around improving relationships with God and each other. While His message never changed, the way He presented it and spoke of it varied according to both His audience and the specific context of the encounter.

Clarity is a vital component of trust-building. Trust is enhanced, deepened, and perpetuated when motives, messages, and options are conveyed with complete transparency. Conversely, insinuations, ulterior motives, and mixed messages destroy trust, which, once broken, is extremely difficult if not impossible to reestablish.

Jesus took responsibility to clearly communicate both the big picture and the details around what He was selling. He invested the time needed to reduce difficult concepts to their simplest form, and organize what He said so His buyers could understand. He accomplished that first by preparing and then initiating dialogue as He taught in private with His disciples, in the synagogues, and in the marketplace with anyone curious enough to engage Him. His preparation assured that what he said would be clear, so that those who listened had the information they needed to contemplate whether or not to buy from Him.

In sales, we craft and deliver messages every day, often without realizing the impact those messages have on others. Every conversation and every written message delivers a meaning that buyers interpret according to their own frame of reference. How do you know if your true intent is being understood by the hearer? You improve the chances of communicating with clarity through diligent preparation, and by setting expectations to foster open dialogue.

Preparation is Often Neglected

In the midst of all the activities that compete for our time and attention, we often disregard the strategic significance of preparing the messages we convey. What we communicate and how we do it have a significant influence on the opinions a buyer forms about us and what we are selling.

Most conversations take place without any type of pre-planning. That is a costly mistake that invites misunderstanding in any conversation, but especially in a sales call. To state the obvious, the objectives of any given conversation can only be achieved if they are known in the first place. Vague or general objectives leave too much room for failure, which can easily be avoided by planning so that you can clearly communicate what you want to accomplish during a sales interaction. That planning should include forming an introductory statement, mapping out key questions that will foster dialogue about the buyer's situation, and preparing the information you want to share.

Jesus spent the first thirty years of His life preparing for a three-year ministry.[6] If you take that ratio at face value, that's ten years of prep for every year of ministry. I have used that ratio of ten to one as a starting point to gauge how much preparation is needed. Does ten to one sound excessive? The good news is, a lot of the preparation time is already done in the form of initial knowledge acquisition resulting in background you can easily draw from. I've found that three to four minutes of preparation for every one minute of dialogue is a good rule of thumb. Be mindful that the shorter the interaction, the more critical the preparation time is.

Jesus also spent time in prayer, tapping into His relationship with God the Father on a regular basis in order to get direction

---

[6] Luke 3:23: "Jesus, assumed to be Joseph's son, was about thirty years old when he began his ministry."

and plan what He was about to do.[7] We can follow suit, incorporating prayer to ask for knowledge, wisdom, and understanding as part of our preparation process.

The Importance of Fostering Dialogue

Jesus lived in a world where almost all communication was verbal, not written. The invention of the internet has led to a dramatic shift away from conversing *with* people to talking *at* people through various electronic methods. My strongly-held bias is that dialoguing with someone in real time, at least by phone or video chat or, even better, face-to-face, is the best way to establish understanding and build trust. Email, text and other messaging programs are effective avenues for quick exchanges of data, recapping conversations, and similar fact-based exchanges. Their major drawback is that they cannot convey the nuances of voice tonality and body language, or extend the benefit of being able to ask questions immediately to clarify understanding before continuing on with the message. The time gaps in electronic communication interrupt the cognitive flow of a conversation and magnify the chances for misinterpretation. Before you have any idea that it's happened, someone takes offense at something they think you said. Now you suffer from someone's judgment against you, based on an assumption or a false premise that you are totally unaware of. Such a misunderstanding in a sales relationship usually ends in the buyer ignoring your attempts to reconnect. It's almost impossible to recover from that, so why not just avoid it altogether by talking to people in real time, where misunderstandings can be addressed and resolved immediately?

---

[7] Luke 5:16: "But Jesus often slipped away from them and went off into the wilderness to pray"; and Luke 6:12: "After this, Jesus went up into the high hills to spend the whole night in prayer to God."

Set Expectations to Establish Rapport

One of the most effective ways to set the stage for clear understanding is to set expectations with the buyer. Jesus was very strategic about doing so. He connected in meaningful ways with people from all different backgrounds, from prestigious politicians and religious leaders to the poorest of the poor. He was able to appeal to men and women, scholars, businessmen, tradesmen, and beggars alike. Considering the wide range of audiences with whom He spoke, His method to connect had to be flexible.

Jesus used various "I have come to..." statements to introduce specific concepts. (See Matthew 5:17, John 6:38, and John 10:10 as examples.[8]) Each of these statements let His audience know more about His mission and what they could expect if they "bought" from Him. In a sales conversation, your version of an "I have come to..." statement is where you create a context for what you want to discuss during the conversation you're about to have. It gives people a frame of reference for the questions you want to ask, helping them know why you're asking, thus increasing their comfort level and willingness to respond honestly.

An example will help illustrate this concept. Let's look at how to set expectations on an initial call-back to a new lead where the goal of the call is to qualify the buyer for a face-to-face meeting. The lead's name is John, and all I know is that he is asking about sales training.

---

[8] Matthew 5:17: "If you think I've come to set aside the law of Moses or the writings of the prophets, you're mistaken. I have come to fulfill and bring to perfection all that has been written"; John 6:38: "And I have come out of heaven not for my own desires, but for the satisfaction of my Father who sent me"; John 10:10: "A thief has one thing in mind—he wants to steal, slaughter, and destroy. But I have come to give you everything in abundance, more than you expect—life in its fullness until you overflow!"

Preparation:

- Research John and the company he works for using your preferred Internet resources. Learn about the industry, and common problems that companies like John's have that you are able to solve.
- Prepare your initial statement to set expectations and direct the flow of the call to its logical next step; i.e. mapping out what happens next or disqualifying John as a prospect. Write it out and practice saying it so it sounds natural.
- Prepare 3-5 thought-provoking questions to generate discussion around things that John might have concerns about.

Make the call:

Me: Hello, John. This is Deb Brown Maher returning your call. I understand you wanted some information about the sales training we offer... (wait for a response)

John: Yes, that's right.

Me: Great! I'm glad you called and am happy to provide the information you want. Here's what I find usually works best: I know you have questions about what we do, how we do it, and what the costs are, right?

John: Yes.

Me: Good. I'm more than happy to answer those questions for you. Also, I'd like to ask you some questions so I can get a full understanding of you and the reason for your call. Would that be okay?

John: Sure!

Me: Thanks, John. I appreciate that. Now, as we talk, we may find there isn't a good fit between your needs and what we do. If so, please don't hesitate to tell me so, and I'll do the same. Okay?

John: No problem.

Me: That's great. On the other hand, we may find that there are some ways I could help. If so, together we'll map out what the next step should be. Does that sound like a good agenda for our call?

John: Perfect.

Me: Awesome. So, I'll ask you to start. What's happening in your world that you are looking for sales training?

To boil down this example to the message behind the words I conveyed:

I have come to:

- orchestrate a dialogue with you so you can get your questions answered.
- get a better understanding of you and your situation.
- help you uncover the performance gap you're experiencing.
- see whether I'm the right person to help you, and if not, I'll be honest and tell you so.

The unspoken messages the buyer hears with this approach are powerful. Some of the feelings that result from being on the receiving end of this are that he knows this salesperson:

- cares enough about me to let me know what I can expect from this conversation.
- cares enough to want to understand the problems I'm having, and won't just start shoving her program down my throat.
- seems sincere in really making sure I get what I need, and if she can't help me, I can say "no" without a fight.
- seems different from other salespeople, and I like how it feels to talk with her.

Taking the time to plan and set expectations paves the way for trust to be established, and when there's trust, great possibilities are set into motion.

℈⇀ Key Points to Remember:

1. Clarity in communication takes time and effort to accomplish.
2. Preparation is critical in helping assure that you say what you need to, in the way that you want to, and that it is received in the way it is intended.
3. Setting expectations allows you to orchestrate the agenda for the conversation, and make the best possible first impression with a buyer.
4. When you make it a habit to set expectations in every stage of the sales process, you demonstrate a consistent and clear message that you are trustworthy and a person of your word.

() Action Steps:

1. The purpose of setting expectations is to clearly define what is about to take place in any given conversation. Think about how you currently start various types of sales interactions (initial call, initial meeting, follow ups, presentations, etc.). Revise your approach to make sure it includes a statement that invites discussion of what's important to the buyer, what you want from the conversation, the possible outcomes (no go, or go on to the next step), and gain agreement before proceeding.
2. Now expand your thinking: Where else could you benefit from setting expectations with a buyer? How could you set expectations prior to discussing their budget, prior to asking for their decision, prior to doing a presentation, to set up a follow up plan, to ask for referrals, etc. Remember, you put people at ease any time you can give them an idea of what to expect before you engage in that topic.
3. Apply the concept of expectation-setting to the end of a sales encounter. How can you set the stage for your next point of contact before you finish the conversation you're in?

4. Get creative and apply this concept to your personal relationships, too. How can you set expectations with:
   a. A child about cleaning their room or doing their homework?
   a. A teenager about the friends that they choose?
   b. Your spouse about making the renovations on your home that you want, or the vacation spot you want to visit?
   c. A neighbor about cleaning up their yard?
   d. Keep going...

Chapter 5

Characteristic #4: Comprehension—Listening, Understanding, and Asking in Order to Serve

⁴⁶After being separated from him for three days, they finally found him in the temple, sitting among the Jewish teachers, listening to them and asking questions. ⁴⁷All who heard Jesus speak were astounded at his intelligent understanding of all that was being discussed and at his wise answers to their questions. (Luke 2:46-47)

The background to this passage is that Jesus, at age 12, traveled to Jerusalem with His parents and their extended family to

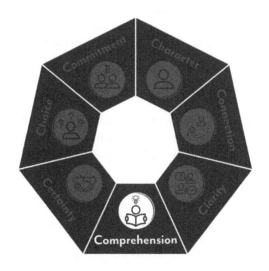

celebrate the Passover festival. Jesus became so engrossed in His conversations with the Jewish teachers in the temple that He literally missed His ride home (the caravan with the entourage from His home town), and His parents had to go back to find Him. Even at that young age, Jesus was demonstrating two critical communication skills that are instrumental to getting extraordinarily beneficial results during sales conversations: listening and asking questions, in that order. The order, listening first before asking questions, is critical.

The Importance of Listening

Consider this: Listening is a gift we can give to others and a valuable way to receive a better understanding of others and what's important to them. Acts 20:35 quotes Jesus as teaching that "Giving brings a far greater blessing than receiving." In Aramaic this phrase is expressed as an idiom that speaks of extravagant generosity: "Blessed are those who try to give more than they've been given."[9] In His willingness to listen to what was important to others, their perspective, ideas, concerns, and desires, Jesus demonstrated His care and concern for them. Every human being has an inherent emotional need to be understood, and we will go to great lengths to satisfy that need. Trust is built quickly when we take the time to listen with the intent of understanding the other person prior to trying to be understood by them.[10]

Leading with a desire to understand others by hearing out their situation before trying to comment on it or help with it demonstrates selflessness, which others sense, appreciate, and

[9] Brian Simmons, The Passion Translation, (Broadstreet Publishing, 2018), 371, Footnote "a"

[10] This concept is expounded on in detail in Stephen R. Covey, The 7 Habits of Highly Effective People: *Powerful Lessons in Personal Change.* (New York: Free Press, 1989), 235.

value. Giving this gift of listening to the other person first also engenders a desire to reciprocate, making people more receptive to hear us when it is our turn to explain what we are selling. True understanding can't be accomplished without listening.

How do you know someone is listening? They make eye contact while you're talking with them. They acknowledge what's been said with comments, or they paraphrase to make sure they are hearing correctly. They ask clarifying questions based on what you said. They don't rush the conversation, look at their watch, or glance at their electronics while you're speaking. They write down things that you say are important to you. All these strategies can be learned and implemented to help us convey that the person speaking to us is important, worth hearing, and deserving of our time and attention.

The Discipline of Observation

We need to listen, not just with our ears, but also with our eyes. Numerous passages in the Gospels mention that Jesus listened and observed before speaking and taking action. One example is when He watched a poor widow who gave all she could in an offering at the Temple in spite of her poverty, before teaching His disciples about the quality of her sacrifice (Mark 12:41-44). A second example is at the wedding in Cana where Jesus turned water into wine only after assessing the predicament the host was in and listening to His mother's advice that He should help fix the situation (John 2:1-9). A third example is found in the story of a crippled man at the pool of Bethesda. Jesus watched how the man behaved before He engaged him in dialogue that led to his being healed of a 38-year long affliction (John 5:6-15). By observing and listening first, Jesus was able to tailor His approach, His questions and His actions, to address the unique need presented in each situation.

Body language, tone of voice, pauses, guttural responses, and even what someone doesn't say, in addition to the words they do say, are all clues we can acknowledge and ask about in order to gain a deeper understanding of the problems each individual wants to solve by buying our product or service. Many salespeople miss these opportunities because they don't understand the value that can be realized by pursuing them. Also, it takes discipline to slow down and ask for this type of clarification. We often get into a hurry to finish the conversation, rather than taking our time to be thorough. Why should we take the time? Because paying attention to the details in what we hear and see, and asking for clarification, allows us to demonstrate empathy, concern, humility, and trustworthiness—things we can't tell someone. We can only show them by our actions.

Questions Are the Answer

Now that you've listened and observed, you are better prepared to ask insightful, thought-provoking questions based on what the buyer cares about, from their perspective, not yours. People buy for their own reasons, not ours. Getting someone to fully explore what it is they want, and what the ideal solution looks like to them, is another gift that salespeople can give to buyers that ultimately builds trust. Here's an example to drive home the difference.

Sell Me A Pen

You may be familiar with the exercise, "Sell Me A Pen," used by many sales managers to evaluate their salespeople's powers of persuasion. Most salespeople, feeling the pressure to perform, will start into a presentation similar to this one:

"Hi there! Did you see this new, sleek, fine-point, easy flow pen that just became available? Let me show you how beautifully it writes," (salesperson starts writing with the pen). "Isn't that great? You need pens for work, for home, in your car, for everything, right? And today, it's only $19.95 for a box of 4!! You can get the pen in blue or black ink, and they're guaranteed to last for 2 years without running out of ink! Isn't that great? How many would you like? Better get them now before they're all gone. They're selling like hot-cakes!!!"

Take a moment and reflect: If you are the buyer, how does that approach make you feel?

Now, here's a different approach modeled on listening, observing, and asking:

"Hi there. Thanks for taking a look at this new pen. I can see that you are curious… What got your attention about it?" [I saw it was something new…]

"Ah, so you're the kind of person who likes new gadgets?" [Yes, I am!]

"Excellent. I'd like to show you what makes this pen special, but before I do, could I ask you some questions to help us both figure out if this is something that would be helpful to you?" [Sure!] Great, thanks.

"Tell me, how much writing do you do?…What's important to you about the way a pen writes?…What do you love about your favorite pen now?…What do you hate about a pen that makes you throw it away?…If you were to buy a 'new' pen, what features are you hoping it will have that you haven't been able to find?"

"Thanks for sharing with me. Based on what you've told me, if this pen can do x, y, and z, it would be of value to you. Is that a fair statement?" [Yes, it is.]

"So, what else do you need to know in order to make a good decision as to whether to purchase one of these new pens today or not?"

Again, reflect on how you feel as the buyer on the receiving end of this approach. What's different?

Compared to the first approach, this one is a two-way conversation, where the salesperson is asking questions to diagnose what is important to the buyer, much like a good physician would do to help figure out what's ailing a patient. Notice that most of the questions start with or include the word "what." Doing so creates an open-ended question, one that requires the person to elaborate, to tell their story in response, vs. giving a closed, yes/no answer. Closed questions are valuable to gather facts and data, but they will not generate the kind of detail that reveals the full extent of the problem that the person is trying to solve.

Also, in this example there is no contrived pressure being brought to bear. Instead, the buyer is invited to express his perspective freely, because the better he can articulate his own needs, the easier it will be to see whether the product at hand is going to meet those needs or not.

What's missing in this static example is the myriad of answers the buyer could give to each of the salesperson's questions. In a live conversation, the information the buyer gives in answer to each question will help the seller decide what to ask next. Using key words from the answers given to formulate the next question guarantees that the conversation stays focused on the buyer's wants, needs, desires, and preferences, and not on the product or service being sold. It's worth pointing out that the price wasn't even brought up in the second illustration, because the value had been revealed through the questioning process.

Successful salespeople make the sales conversation about the person, not the product or price.

One of the most liberating benefits of this approach is that the salesperson has no pressure to convince the buyer of anything. The only pressure the salesperson should feel is that which prompts him/her to orchestrate an interaction where the buyer feels safe enough to be honest, because that honesty makes it possible to get the best possible outcome for both parties. When the buyer has a need that the seller can meet, a sale takes place and both parties benefit. When the buyer's need is not resolved by the seller's product or service, no sale takes place and both parties understand why. Any form of win-lose as a final outcome will always damage the relationship, whether in the short-term with back-outs or bitter feelings, or in the long-run when future sales are forfeited because of negative reviews.

Presentations Are Over-rated

Without understanding the importance of listening, observing, and asking, salespeople have little choice but to focus on presenting features and benefits from their own perspective. Yes, sales are made that way. But it is clear that there's a better way, one that offers a path to mutual gain.

There does come a time when it is appropriate to share information about your products or services, how they work, and the potential outcomes they could achieve for the buyer. Traditional sales training courses emphasize the importance of delivering a well-polished "sales presentation" (the pitch) in which the salesperson informs the buyer of all the reasons they should love what is being offered. As we saw in the previous example, if the information is presented from the seller's perspective, there is a disconnect with the buyer. Remember, people buy for their own reasons, not ours. It doesn't matter how I see it; if they don't see it my way, no amount of well-polished convincing will work. The buyer alone holds the power to convince herself to buy. The salesperson holds the power to craft the discussion around problems and solutions, only revealing features and benefits that mean something to the buyer at the appropriate time in the conversation.

Presenting information without tailoring it to the individual buyer's unique needs leaves too much room for unanswered questions, and the buyer will find a way to say no, directly or in the form of "I want to think it over," or "I'll get back to you." At that point, you've lost their trust and they seem to disappear, never returning your attempts to reconnect with them. It is worth noting that in the Christian community we have a name for this presentation-without-tailoring as well: Proselytizing. Proselytizing—trying to convince someone to believe in Jesus—is as ineffective as trying to convince people to buy through a sales pitch. That's why Jesus simply didn't proselytize—or pitch. What He did instead was evangelize; He shared the good news in a way that resonated with each individual He addressed.

Tailoring the Presentation to Serve the Buyer

Jesus recognized that the message that resonates is the message that is personalized. Instead of sharing a generic, one-size-fits-all message with His followers, the Gospels tell us that no two conversations Jesus had during His ministry were the same. There was no "canned speech," no convenient catchphrase, no "three-easy-steps" summation.

Translating client messages about the problems they need to solve into meaningful solution statements requires the ability to synthesize the information a buyer has shared and present the features of your product or service back to her as answers to her problems, using language that explains the "what's in it for me" (WIIFM) from the angle of her unique need.

Jesus customized each conversation, and we can do the same. He spoke with Simon and his brother Andrew in the language of fishermen (Matthew 4:18-20), and debated the Pharisees and Sadducees through the logic of the teachers of the law (Matthew 22). From the blind man to the adulterous woman, and from the Jews to the Romans, Jesus was engaged in building intense personal relationships which were the key to His ministry. People heard and received His message because He cared enough to answer the WIIFM (what's in it for me) for each person He met. He recognized the inherent reality of the human condition and did not hesitate to address people directly with answers befitting their unique circumstances. For example, what was in it for the leper in the story in Mark 1:40-45? A miraculous healing of his leprosy, which allowed him to reenter society and regain his life. What was in it for the adulterous woman whom the Pharisees wanted to stone to death in John 8:1-11? Forgiveness and freedom from the bonds of a self-destructive lifestyle. Even the rich young ruler in Matthew 19:16-26 was given a clear answer to the question of what was in it for him: the ability not only to inherit eternal life in heaven, but also to experience the freedom of moving beyond worldly possessions and serving the poor in this life as well.

When someone is looking to buy something, you can be certain that their main focus is always, "how will I benefit if I make this purchase?" Jesus knew that, and He didn't shy away from crafting meaningful and specific "presentations" that met each person where they were, and then showing them a way to get where they wanted to go by "buying" from Him. His "product" and "service" didn't change, but His approach to each person did.

When you have these types of discussions with people, it will change your conversations from product-focused to people-focused, from trying to convince someone to buy to helping people make the best decision about purchasing—for themselves. Remember that you are a decision gatherer; they are the decision maker. Keep that straight and you're well on your way to transforming the way you sell.

ℴ→ Key Points to Remember:

1. Listening and observing fosters relevant and meaningful dialogue. Dialogue integrates questions and answers that promote mutual understanding. Mutual understanding opens the door to agreement on a course of action. Listening + Dialogue + Q&A + Mutual Understanding + Agreed Course of Action = Buy-In

2. If you're talking, you aren't listening.

3. Thinking about what you're going to say next also stops you from listening.

4. Listening with the intent of understanding takes effort! It requires focus and discipline to think only about what the person is saying and trying to understand what he means by the words he uses.

5. Listening involves eyes as well as ears, to observe non-verbal clues, to hear beyond the words to the true meaning.

6. Listening fosters understanding, trust, respect, and honesty.

7. People buy for their reasons, not ours.

8. People buy solutions to problems in order to prevent or eliminate pain.

9. Pain is personal, and only the buyer can decide the ultimate value he will receive if that pain is eliminated.

10. Questions are the answer. Questions that start with "Tell me more about…" or "What…" will encourage the buyer to share her story so we are better positioned to sell her what she truly needs, or explain how our solution falls short.

11. The buyer is the decision maker. The salesperson is responsible to get a decision.

◊ Action Steps:

Think about applying these exercises in work or personal relationships before experimenting during a sales call to build your skill and confidence that they work.

1. Talk less, listen more.
   a. Start by observing your own behavior for a day.
   b. What percentage of your conversations are you talking, listening, observing, asking questions?
   c. Pick one thing that you want to implement, and put it into action. Track how often you are successful.
   d. Take note of how others react to you as you implement your new approach.
   e. Make adjustments to get better results going forward.

2. Seek first to understand. Try to understand the other person's perspective before you try to get him to see it your way.
   a. First, become aware of when you are imposing your ideas, opinion, or method on others.
   b. Then figure out what you could ask to get their perspective on that subject before you share your thoughts.
   c. Adjust what you share according to the information you have obtained by asking even just one question prior to speaking.
   d. Record your observations prior to and after the conversation. What did you learn?

3. Practice being more curious—more inquisitive, intrigued, interested—in what others think and say. Here are some ways you can do that:
   a. Ask them, "Tell me more about that…"
   b. Ask them, "What is your thought process around [what they just shared]?
   c. Ask them, "Would you elaborate on how important [what they just said] is to you?
   d. Ask them, "Why did you pick x and not y [another choice]?
   e. Do a mental review of what you learned from that person that you didn't know before. How does knowing that help your relationship with that person? What

adjustments can you make to continue to deepen that relationship?

4. Change your closed-ended questions to open-ended questions:

    a. Instead of asking your child, "How was school today?" and getting the typical answer, "Fine," change it to, "What was the best thing that happened today at school?" Or "What was the hardest thing that you witnessed today at school?" Or pick your own open-ended question and try it out.

    b. No children? Try it out on your significant other: "What was the best thing that happened today?" Or "What was the hardest thing that you witnessed today?" Or pick your own open-ended question and try it out.

    c. Take note of the responses you get from your different approach, and make adjustments to continue to foster more open dialogue.

Chapter 6

Characteristic #5: Certainty— Building Trust and Showing that You Care

⁵Life is good for the one who is generous and charitable, conducting affairs with honesty and truth. ⁶Their circumstances will never shake them and others will never forget their example. (Psalm 112:5-6)

When we behave in a generous, kind, and loving way toward others, conducting our affairs with honesty and truth, we foster good relationships and also reap the rewards of doing so. Jesus modeled giving to others. He gave first, and provided all who chose to buy in to His message a clear, honest picture of what they could expect from Him in return, including what it would

cost. He created an environment of certainty based on honest and truthful interactions.

Certainty is defined as the quality of being reliably true. We humans crave certainty, wanting to be able to trust people and situations to be reliable, valid, factual, and sure. We have the opportunity to strategically create an environment of trust, even with complete strangers, by how we conduct ourselves. The reason it is so important to build trust with a potential buyer is because of the inherent feelings of uncertainty that both buyer and seller experience as they engage in a sales conversation.

Put yourself in the buyer's shoes. You have a very real problem you're trying to solve and you aren't sure if the salesperson has the right solution. You're concerned about making a mistake by choosing the wrong vendor. You don't trust that just any salesperson will look out for your best interest, so you withhold information in an effort to self-protect. You do your best to be as knowledgeable as possible so you don't get misled, but you don't know what you don't know.

Now put yourself in the salesperson's shoes. You don't know the buyer, or the real reason they have engaged you in a conversation about your product or service. You have no idea whether they have the resources and are willing to invest them to buy your solution. You aren't sure you're talking to all the decision makers or when they might actually be placing an order. It's hard to trust everything the buyer says because buyers have lied to you in the past, and sales you thought were a sure thing fell through.

No matter which seat you're in, feelings of uncertainty abound, triggering anxiety and a sense of vulnerability that bias both buyer and seller toward skepticism and distrust that can destroy rapport and kill sales opportunities quickly.

Every buyer wants to know two things from the seller: "Are you able to help me?" and, "Can I trust you?" Rarely are these questions asked directly, because even when the answers are "yes and yes," buyers still don't trust you *because* you're a salesperson. The only way to earn people's trust is to *show* that you are trustworthy and prove by your actions and your words that you are different from the stereotypical "pushy salesperson" they are expecting you to be.

Show that You Are Trustworthy

Let's take a closer look at four ways that Jesus modeled trust-building behaviors so we can identify specific actions He took and apply them to sales conversations.

1. *Do what you say you're going to do.*

This uncomplicated strategy may do more to impact trust-building than any other that you do for the simple reason that you have abundant opportunities to demonstrate it. Jesus was a man of His word, always doing what He said. Because He was the Son of God, He often demonstrated His words through miracles, and those miracles helped His audience arrive at a state of trusting Him with their eternal allegiance. Good news for us: we don't have to perform miracles to get our audience's attention (although some might say they've experienced a miracle when their salesperson actually listened to them more than they talked!). We just have to give our word and then keep it.

From your very first interaction with someone, you can prove you are a person of your word by doing the following:

- When you set expectations for the conversation, and then follow those expectations.
- When you ask the buyer how much time she has for the meeting, and then offer to stop the meeting when that time limit has been met.
- When you say you'll get back to someone with specific information by a certain date and you do it.

- When you say your solution will perform in certain ways and it does.
- When you promise to modify your solution to meet someone's unique needs and you follow through on that promise.
- When you offer references and then deliver them promptly.

You get the idea. Give your word and follow through on it. Remember, also, never offer to do anything that you aren't prepared to follow through on, because nothing breaks trust more quickly than breaking your word.

2. *Believe in what you are selling.*

Your product or service is the deliverable that you sell, but the message that builds trust with others is your confidence that the solution you offer is able to improve their quality of life. If you don't believe in what you're selling, your words and actions *will* reveal it because beliefs drive behavior. Although it is possible to behave in a way that compromises one's beliefs, contradicting your beliefs takes an emotional toll and is difficult to sustain long-term. When you are confident in the value your solution provides, you speak with certainty that your solution has potential to help the person you're engaged with. Your belief in your solution helps the buyer trust and believe that you can provide the solution that he needs.

When approached by two blind men, Jesus had to believe He could perform the miracle that was being asked of Him, as did the recipients, or He could not have delivered the miracle:

27As Jesus left the house, two blind men began following him, shouting out over and over, "Son of David, show us mercy and heal us!" 28And they followed him right into the house where Jesus was staying. So Jesus asked them, "Do you believe that I have the power to restore sight to your eyes?" They replied, "Yes Lord, we believe!" 29Then Jesus put his hands over their eyes and said,

"You will have what your faith expects!" [30]*And instantly their eyes opened—they could see!...* (Matthew 9:27-30a)

Jesus was able to respond the way He did because He believed He could deliver the expected results.

3. *Be transparent about the costs as well as the benefits.*

Jesus displayed transparency many times. Often, it was to make sure His audience knew the cost-benefit ratio of His offering. One example was when He said, "Expect to be hated by all because of my name, but be faithful to the end and you will experience life and deliverance" (Matthew 10:22). In that statement Jesus set clear expectations with no sugar coating. His followers knew both the cost and the benefit if they said "yes" to following Him. Notice that He first spoke of the price they'd have to pay, and ended with the benefits, rather than the other way around. If people were going to "buy" from Him, He wanted them to know both what was required of them, as well as the rewards they would receive.

You can impact a buyer's attitude towards you by setting realistic expectations at the outset of each interaction, as we discussed in chapter 4. It is also helpful to set expectations any time a buyer indicates the desire for something from you that you aren't able or willing to provide. One example from my own experience involves meeting with a prospect, whom I'll call Jane, about sales coaching to improve her closing ratios. Jane shared that she was looking for someone who would "hound" her (her word) to make the changes that would enable her to reach her goals. Because I know it is human nature to rebel against hounding, I needed to address the issue immediately, testing to see what she really meant by her comment.

Deb: Jane, I find it interesting that you want someone to hound you to make sure you do the things you commit to implementing. As a sales coach, I certainly do have conversations with people about their progress toward their goals. But hounding...? Can

I ask you, how has it worked out for you in the past when you had someone hounding you to get things done?

Jane: "Hmmmmm. Well, it works in the beginning, and then I get tired of it and start to feel stupid, so I give up. Come to think of it, I'm still trying improve my closing ratio."

Deb: Thanks for your honesty about that, Jane. If we could work together to figure out a better way to get to your desired goals, and for you to be able to sustain that performance long-term, would you be open to exploring that?

Jane: That would be great!

Deb: Super. Let's start by looking at a time in your past when you were successful at reaching your goals. What behaviors were you doing consistently that helped you then?

Notice the familiar pattern we discussed in chapter 2 applied here: acknowledge, affirm, and shift direction with a question. Asking Jane to evaluate past results when someone hounded her caused her to quickly convince herself that it didn't work so well, and she became open to the possibility of exploring alternatives.

Now let's consider what it would sound like if Jane's response went the other way.

Deb: Jane, I appreciate that you want someone to hound you to do the things you want to implement. As a coach, I certainly do have conversations with people about their progress toward their goals. But hounding…? Can I ask you, how has it worked out for you in the past when you had someone hounding you to get things done?

Jane: It's worked pretty well. I do best when I have someone reminding me constantly of what I should be doing, and calling me out on it every day until I change.

Deb: So, it has worked for you. I'm curious, then, what has changed that you find yourself in need of help again now?

Jane: Well, I don't have someone looking over my shoulder, so I've gotten off track. I just need someone to stay on me and all will be well.

Deb: Thanks for sharing that, Jane. What if I could help you figure out a better way to get to your desired goals and put safeguards in place that reduce the likelihood of backsliding into old habits?

Jane: No, I really want someone who will push me every day.

Deb: I hear you. Thanks for your honesty, and allow me to return the favor of being straight with you, too: I have a problem. It's my problem not yours. I'm just not set up to do what you're asking, so if that's a show-stopper for you, we should probably end our conversation here, no?"

Jane: You're right. Thanks for taking the time to come see me today.

Deb: Absolutely! Before I leave, can I ask you, what would have to change in your world for you to want to connect with me again?

Jane: Well, if I get into a bind and what I'm doing doesn't work, we could revisit this conversation.

Deb: Would you want me to touch base with you at some point in the future just to check in and see how things are going for you?

Jane: Sure, call me in 6 months and ask me how it's going.

Deb: I'll do that. And if anything changes sooner, don't hesitate to give me a call and we'll talk it through.

Jane: I will. Thank you!

As soon as I realize Jane is not willing to consider working the way I know could help her best, I ask if it's time to end our conversation, purposely allowing her to make the decision either to stop, or to keep going. Sometimes, when you demonstrate the willingness to stand your ground and stick to the process you know works best, the prospect changes her mind and becomes open to exploring a different way. If not, the interaction is over and neither of us have to endure the inevitable, uncomfortable values clash that would ensue. Think about it: if I didn't stand my ground, and took her on as a client anyway, I'd have purchased trouble because I'd be agreeing to do something that I know isn't good for either of us in the long run. Since I'm a person of my word, I'd be boxing myself into doing work that I hated, and that never works out well for anyone. Being transparent about my methods, and letting her decide, set the stage for an open and honest relationship, whether we work together or not. Because I was honest, should Jane change her mind in the future, she will be comfortable contacting me to re-open our discussion.

The benefits of building trust in this way extend beyond the immediate transaction. In both scenarios, trust is established, mutual respect is given, and the door to continue in the relationship is left open, should things change in the future.

4. *Never compromise.*

Certainty about what Jesus stood for didn't always result in agreement with Him. It meant that the buyer could trust that "what you see is what you get"; no hidden motives, no manipulation, no bait and switch. Jesus never swayed from His ways, even when the brightest and most powerful members of society tried to trap Him with their cunning. A great example of this is the passage about paying taxes to Caesar:

13Then they [the chief priests, religious scholars and leaders] sent a delegation of Pharisees, together with some staunch supporters of Herod, to entrap Jesus with his own words. 14So they approached him and said, "Teacher, we know that you're an honest man of integrity and you teach us the truth of God's ways. We can clearly see that you're not one who speaks only to win the people's favor, because you speak the truth without regard to the consequences. So tell us, then, what you think. Is it proper for us to pay taxes to Caesar or not?" 15Jesus saw through their hypocrisy and said to them, "Why are you testing me? Show me one of the Roman coins." 16They brought him a silver coin used to pay the tax. "Now, tell me," Jesus said, "whose head is on this coin and whose inscription is stamped on it?" "Caesar's," they replied. 17Jesus said, "Precisely. The coin bears the image of the emperor Caesar, so you should pay the emperor his portion. But because you bear the image of God, you must give back to God all that belongs to him." And they were utterly stunned by Jesus' words. (Mark 12:13-17)

Even those testing Jesus recognized the truth about His character when they stated, in verse 14, "Teacher, we know that you're an honest man of integrity and you teach us the truth of God's ways. We can clearly see that you're not one who speaks only to win the people's favor, because you speak the truth without regard to the consequences." They were hoping to use that quality of truth-telling they claimed to admire so much as a weapon against Him, but their plan failed when Jesus used the strategies we've already discussed in the previous chapter: He listened, observed, asked questions, and only after hearing their answers did He offer any reply. His calculated reply spoke to the heart of the matter, the essence of what was being asked: give allegiance where it is due. With that response, Jesus was able to stand His ground on what He believed, speak the truth without compromise or criticism, and subsequently leave a positive impression on all those who heard the interchange, even His challengers. Those who challenged Jesus so vehemently never did buy in to His teachings, but through this and other similar displays of consistency and steadfast character, He did win the trust and allegiance of many.

In summary, it is important to remember that we are either building trust or suspicion, certainty or fear. There is no middle ground when it comes to this, and it takes a conscious effort on our part to shape conversations so both buyer and seller get the best possible outcome to every conversation.

☞ Key Points to Remember:

1. Buyers *and* sellers enter the sales conversation with an inherent distrust, based on negative past experiences. This can be overcome by purposely behaving in ways that build trust.
2. Four specific ways to build trust quickly are to:
   a. Be a person of your word by doing what you say you will do.
   b. Believe in what you are selling.
   c. Be transparent about costs as well as benefits.
   d. Never compromise your values.
3. Jesus models how we can stand up to the most skeptical buyer without bullying or backing down, but rather standing our ground and staying true to what we believe.

⟨⟩ Action Steps:

1. List three ways that you have built trust with buyers in the past. For example, "I always share an agenda with the buyer." Or, "I never bad-mouth my competitors." Or, "I take ownership whenever I have misstated something." How can you use those strategies more often? Write down your answers and build on your ideas as you give trust-building more thought over the next days and weeks.
2. List three new ways you can build trust with prospects based on what you've read in this chapter. What do you need to learn and practice in order to put those ideas into action? Where can you get the input that you need?
3. Think about ways that you have compromised your own values in the past, and recall the negative consequences

of doing so. What do you have to do differently to avoid making similar compromises in the future?

4. Ask someone you trust to give you candid feedback on how well you build trust. Share what you're doing to get better at it, and ask that person for any pointers that will help you.

Chapter 7

Characteristic #6: Choice—Choose to Serve Others and Give Others Choices

In everything you do, be careful to treat others in the same way you'd want them to treat you, for that is the essence of all the teachings of the Law and the Prophets. (Matthew 7:12)

The greatest among you will be the one who always serves others from the heart. (Matthew 23:11)

How we treat others is a choice. Offering others the freedom to decide what is best for them is also a choice we make. It is a choice to grant others the right to choose.

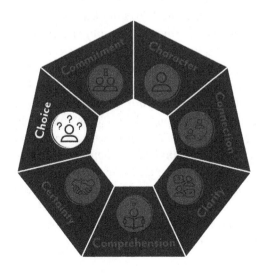

Jesus' life work revolved around serving others, and those who bought in to His message willingly decided to pay the price to receive what He offered. His greatest joy was to see those He ministered to get what they wanted and needed. To those who said "no," the option to buy in could be revisited anytime any of them changed their mind. Serving others requires a conscious decision to deny self, to elevate their needs above our own. It also involves a choice to give unconditionally, without expectation of anything in return. Don't get me wrong: you do have the right to get paid for your products and services when they are the right solution for the buyer. What I'm saying is that your mindset drives your actions, so if you *only* give because you want something in return, it will show, and you'll alienate people who otherwise would have bought from you.

Jesus taught on this subject of putting others ahead of ourselves, and the benefits of doing so, while at a Sabbath day meal hosted by a prominent Jewish religious leader. There was disagreement over who should be seated where:

[7]*When Jesus noticed how the guests for the meal were all vying for the seats of honor, he shared this story with the guests around the table:* [8]*"When you are invited to an important social function, don't be quick to sit near the head of the table, choosing the seat of honor. What will happen when someone more distinguished than you arrives?* [9]*The host will then bring him over to where you are sitting and ask for your seat, saying in front of all the guests, 'You're in the wrong place. Please give this person your seat.' Disgraced, you will have to take whatever seat is left.* [10]*Instead, when you're invited to a banquet, you should choose to sit in the lowest place so that when your host comes and sees you there, he may say, 'My friend, come with me and let me seat you in a better place.' Then, in front of all the other guests at the banquet, you will be honored and seated in the place of highest respect.* [11]*Remember this: everyone with a lofty opinion*

of who he is and who seeks to raise himself up will be humbled before all. And everyone with a modest opinion of who he is and chooses to humble himself will be raised up before all."
(Luke 14:7-11)

In this teaching, Jesus clearly states the benefits of choosing to take last place in order to honor someone else. This is what verses 8-10 might sound like when applied to a sales encounter:

(8) When you are meeting a prospect for an important sales call, don't be quick to boast about how much your offerings will help them. What would happen when they talk to another vendor who shows more concern for their well-being than you have? (9) The buyer not only won't hire you, he will also spread negative comments about you. (10) Instead, when you are having an important sales conversation, be humble. Don't assume you know what someone needs. Listen to the buyer, ask questions to understand what is important to him, and only offer a presentation when you and he are convinced you have the right solution to his problem. Then the buyer will reward you by hiring you, and telling his friends about how much you have helped him.

Reaping the Rewards of Selflessness

The counterintuitive benefit of this service-motivated, other-centered approach is that when someone realizes that you've put their needs first, it prompts them to reciprocate.[11] They

---

[11] The law of reciprocity is found in Luke 6:37-38: Jesus said, "Forsake the habit of criticizing and judging others, and then you will not be criticized and judged in return. Don't look at others and pronounce them guilty, and you will not experience guilty accusations yourself. Forgive over and over and you will be forgiven over and over. Give generously and generous gifts will be given back to you, shaken down to make room for more. Abundant gifts will pour out upon you with such an overflowing measure that it will run over the top! Your measurement of generosity becomes the measurement of your return."

start looking for ways to give back to you, including being more honest and vulnerable in describing their real needs, and looking for ways to justify doing business with you even when your prices are higher than the competition. That is the environment where mutual benefit is born, when both parties look to do what is best for each other. We have the power to initiate that beneficial cascade. Our selfless act is a spark that the buyer either fans to a flame or puts out, for whatever reason. It is always the buyer's choice whether to reciprocate, and whether to buy or not. As long as we set the stage to achieve mutual benefit, and pursue the conversation to its mutually beneficial conclusion, we have done our part.

Asking for the Sale

As a salesperson, it *is* our responsibility to ask the buyer to make a decision whether or not to buy from us. How we do that is critical to maintaining the buyer's right to choose. When we keep in mind that the buyer is the decision-maker, and we are a decision-gatherer, we demonstrate respect and foster trust. People who use hard-sell tactics violate this principle by trying to convince people to buy. *They ask for the "yes" instead of asking for a decision, yes or no, disregarding the buyer's right to choose.* The following true story illustrates how the hard-sell strategy systematically denies the buyer the right to choose.

My husband and I decided to replace the roof of our house. We had no idea what it might cost, so when a flyer came in the mail from a company that said they were doing work for a neighbor, we decided to set up an appointment. At the appointed day and time, the salesperson arrived, made himself comfortable at our kitchen table, and began his show-and-tell presentation. For 45 minutes he didn't ask any questions except the insulting ones designed for him to "collect yeses." He directed everything he said toward my husband, making no eye contact with me, and bragged about how successful the company was, and the quality of the materials they used. Then came a 15-minute smoke-and-mirrors explanation of "the price," showing other houses like ours and what their roofs cost. The starting number for our roof was $17,500. As he explained various incentives, collecting a yes after each one, the price came down to $11,500, but only if we signed right that minute. He warned that if he left the house without a deposit, the price would be $17,500 when we called back.

After enduring his condescending attitude for about an hour, I couldn't take any more and told him we would not be signing anything that evening. I asked him to leave, to which he replied, "Dear, you're stupid if you say no to this deal." Yes, his first word spoken to me was "dear," followed by calling me stupid!

It was over. We escorted him out the door and questioned our sanity for putting up with him as long as we did. Just so I don't leave you with a cliff-hanger, we ended up hiring a wonderful company who did great job on our roof for—are you ready?—$6,200. And they weren't the lowest price quote we received. For us it was more important to have trust in the people doing the work, and knowing that we could call them if any problems arose in the future. Value is always defined by the buyer.

Table 7.1, on the next page gives a comparative list of the offensive, high-pressure tactics that elicited a guaranteed "no" from us, and their service-motivated, other-centered behavior counterparts.

To summarize, the hard-sell approach is focused on the salesperson's wants and needs, and is disrespectful of others. To sell like Jesus means putting others first, learning what's important to them, offering them a choice, and then being at peace with whatever they decide, so that the relationship is preserved regardless of the outcome.

Table 7.1   Comparative list of high-pressure and service-motivated sales tactics.

High-pressure sales	Service-motivated sales
Assumes	Seeks to understand
Manipulates	Influences respectfully
Demands	Offers choices
Intimidates	Assists
Discounts you, your knowledge, your perspective	Affirms you, your knowledge, your perspective
Suspicious	Trusting
Knows-it-all	Curious, open to learning
Tells	Asks
Decides for you	Allows you to decide
Only accepts a "yes"	A well-qualified "no" is okay, as is a "yes"

Practical Ways to Take the Other-centered Position

Here are three examples to help you see the contrast between these two approaches:

1. Buyer's question: *"How much does your solution cost?"* (when asked too early in the sales process)

Hard-sell answer: It's only $1995, and with that you get x, y, and z, and you'll be able to brag to all your friends that you have the newest, latest, greatest.

Other-centered response: "I appreciate that you need to budget for this expenditure, and we will certainly talk about the cost of our solution if it makes sense to do so. At this point in our conversation, I don't understand your unique situation well enough to even guess at what the best solution for you is, let alone what it might cost. Could we start by discussing the challenges you're facing, and make sure that there is a good match between what you need and what we can provide?"

2. Buyer's question: *Can you send me some literature?*

Hard-sell answer: "Sure, I'll send it right over to you." Seller proceeds by sending what he thinks the buyer needs to see to convince the buyer to make a purchase.

Other-centered response: "I'd be happy to. Help me out; we have a lot of different things I could send. What were you hoping to see in the literature, so I can narrow it down and send you the right thing?" Proceed to engage the buyer in dialogue so you can uncover the true concerns the buyer was hoping to read about, or uncover that the buyer really isn't interested at all, and was just being polite by asking for literature.

3. Buyer's question: *"Tell me about what you do."*

Hard-sell answer: "Sure!" followed by a 'dog and pony' information dump.

Other-centered response: "I'd be happy to share all about what we do, how we do it and what it costs. Before I do, it would be helpful to hear from you, so I don't spout off a bunch of information that isn't important to you. What is it that's pressing on you that you were hoping we could help with?"

Recognize the familiar pattern in the other-centered responses? Acknowledge, affirm, and shift direction with a question. This strategy works anytime the buyer is asking for something you can't answer because you don't yet have enough information about what the buyer values in order to respond intelligently.

Ask Questions that Drive Self-discovery

If you have a problem you're trying to solve, which would you prefer:

a. Have someone to tell you what the problem is and how you should fix it? or,

b. Have someone help *you* figure out what the problem is, and how *you* want to fix it?

What's the difference? In a., the answer comes from the *outside in*. In b., it comes from the *inside out*. It's human nature to want to "do it yourself" because there is an undeniable satisfaction and a sense of control that comes when we discover something for ourselves. The questions that you ask during the sales call help buyers figure out both the seriousness of their problem and what they are ultimately willing to do to get the right fix. They own their problem, and they get to decide how they want to fix it—with your guidance—if they'll allow it.

Below is a list of diagnostic questions that help people understand their own situation at a deeper level. These questions lead to greater awareness of the full magnitude of the situation and the corresponding value of the solution they seek. Asking questions that help them self-diagnose shows your desire to understand *them*, and that fosters trust. It also keeps you from being in the position of pointing out their problems. No one likes to be wrong. So, although it often seems easier to tell a buyer what the problem is and how the features and benefits of your solution will help him or her, you risk alienating the buyer by doing so. Asking diagnostic questions takes time, effort, and courage, but is well worth it for the trust it builds and the higher quality of sales it produces.

No matter what you are selling, these questions (modified to your circumstances) will help you guide your prospects to uncover the full impact of the gap they are solving for:

- What caused you to start looking for [insert your product/service here] at this particular point in time? (This uncovers any precipitating event that triggered the need.)

- How long have you been dealing with this issue? (The longer they've suffered, the more it hurts.)
- What have you done in the past to try to fix it? (If nothing, you'll be the first to help them.)
- If they've done something, ask, "How did that work?" (You want to find out what went wrong that they are still looking for a fix.)
- What would you say it has cost you to still be dealing with this issue? (Inaction always has tangible and intangible costs.)
- What's kept you from making changes prior to this? (Differing opinions about what to do? Lack of budget? Denial?)
- What is the ideal solution in your mind? (Get them to envision what "good" looks like.)
  - Has it ever been that way? (Did they have it and lose it, or did they never have it?)
    - [If it was,] What changed?
    - [If it wasn't] Do you believe it can be fixed? (If not, it's an uphill battle. If yes, they probably have some ideas of how but need help executing.)
- What are you hoping I would be able to do for you? (Get them to articulate their expectations of the company they will eventually hire so you can see if their needs are within your scope.)
- When do you need a solution to be in place? (Gathers information to determine capacity to deliver.)
- What kind of budget/resources are you willing to allocate to implement a solution? (Gathers information about the ability to pay and willingness to change.)
- Who besides yourself is part of the decision-making process to put a solution in place? (Gathers information about who, how, and when a decision will be made.)

- What has to change at your end to successfully implement a solution like this one? (Helps them think through the process of change that buying a solution will trigger.)

This list comes with a strong warning. It is *not* to be used as a checklist, asking one question, then the next on down the list. Rather, it is a framework of questions that shape your sales conversation, helping you uncover the buyer's reasons to buy and whether there is a good fit between what the buyer wants and what you can deliver. In real life, the buyer's answer to each one of these questions will lead to a cascade of follow-up questions that relate specifically to the answer that was given. Here's an example using the first question from the list above with sales training as the product being sold:

Question: What caused you to start looking for [sales training] at this particular point in time?

Answer: We just got our mid-year results and we're trending to hit only 70% of our target. We have to do something now to try to hit our numbers for the year.

Follow-up question: That sounds like it could be a challenge. May I ask, what percent to target have you historically achieved at the mid-year point?

Notice that the second question is formed using information contained in the buyer's answer (70% to target), acknowledging the problem, and asking for more information to gain a deeper understanding of whether what is happening this year is an anomaly, or a pattern. Again, the answer to this question will contain information that helps form the next question, and so forth. Some or all of the remaining diagnostic questions can be brought into the conversation as and when it makes sense to do so. Each one will evoke a series of follow-on questions until you have all the information you need to talk about their budget and decision making process.

Addressing the Pain to Change

Whether buyers realize it or not, they are buying the need to *change* in addition to whatever product or service you are selling. Implementing anything different from the status quo requires change. No matter how compelling the reasons to buy, change is always difficult. Jesus clearly stated the changes needed if someone wanted to follow Him when He said: "If you truly desire to be my disciple, you must disown your life completely, embrace my 'cross' as your own, *and surrender to my ways*" (Luke 9:23). In short, to follow Jesus, things had to change dramatically by surrendering one's self-centered desires. Not everyone is willing to pay that price. Not every buyer is willing to pay the price of change that will lead to successful implementation of your solution, either.

When you take the time to help people diagnose the full extent of their situation, the money needed to pay for your offering is rarely the main reason you get a "no." More often it is the requisite willingness to change that the buyer, or others at the company, are not willing to make. Therefore, resistance to change is best dealt with during the sales process. If not, it can sabotage your implementation and cause buyer's remorse, returns, and negative reviews.

Finally, why raise the need for change with a buyer? I'll answer with another question: When is the last time a salesperson helped you think through the ramifications of change before trying to get your money? Almost never, right? You can set yourself apart in the marketplace and make more sales by doing so.

Make the Shift from Information Giver to Information Gatherer

When you take the time to help others understand their own situation more fully, learning about it yourself in the process, you empower them to make a well-informed decision about how to proceed. Because you've orchestrated this type of dialogue, the buyer automatically assumes you are able to solve the problem that was uncovered, and often times no presentation is needed. Also, if at any point in the conversation you realize that you can't provide what the buyer needs, you can be honest and say so, allowing the buyer to decide to look elsewhere. This is the arena where you orchestrate mutual benefit and you are positioned, then, to reap the rewards of doing so.

☞ Key Points to Remember:

1. We have a choice to be other-centered or self-centered in how we approach each sales conversation.
2. The buyer always has the right to choose, to make an independent decision whether or not to buy.
3. Putting the needs of others ahead of our own allows us to tap into the law of reciprocity,[12] opening the door to receive even more than we gave.
4. The diagnostic questioning process puts the power to identify problems in the hands of the person experiencing them.
5. No one else can convince anyone of anything. You can only convince yourself, and to do that you need facts.
6. The buyer's pain is personal, and how he defines "value" is the only definition that matters.
7. Diagnostic questions help the buyer uncover for himself what is really important to him and what he is willing to do to get the solution that he seeks.
8. The pain of change is real, and is responsible for stopping many deals from going through. You can initiate a discussion about the pain to change, and help the buyer come to terms with, and sell her colleagues on, whatever change is required to obtain the benefits that they seek.

---

[12] Ibid.

() Action Steps:

Practicing these strategies with family members is a great way to refine your skills before trying them with a prospect.

1. Review Table 7.1 (high-pressure vs. service-motivated sales characteristics). What are you doing now? What aren't you doing that you could incorporate into your sales approach? Choose one strategy, identify one action you can take toward that strategy and start incorporating it into your conversations. For example: instead of assuming that I know what someone means by a certain phrase they used (We need to move on this soon.), ask them to elaborate and clarify. (By soon you mean...?).

2. Identify ways that you may be trying to convince people to do things, instead of helping them decide if it's something they want to do. For example: I recently tried to convince a friend to get out of her comfort zone, listing all the great reasons that she should. She resisted, strongly. I switched my approach to ask her "What do you think you should do?" She answered quickly with her idea, which I was then able to support.

3. Review the list of diagnostic questions under the section, "Ask Questions that Drive Self-discovery." Which ones are you already using? Which ones could you add to your sales conversations? Pick one that you think will help you the most and start asking it in any situation where it seems to fit. Take note of the results, modify your approach based on the feedback you get, and try again. Send me your success stories at deb@debbrownsales.com.

Chapter 8

Characteristic #7
Commitment—Delivery and Follow-up

¹*Jesus left them and went again into the synagogue, where he encountered a man who had an atrophied, paralyzed hand. ²Everyone was watching Jesus closely to see if he would heal the man on the Sabbath, giving them a reason to accuse him of breaking Sabbath rules. ³Jesus said to the man with the paralyzed hand, "Stand here in the middle of the room." ⁴Then he turned to all those gathered there and said, "Which is it? Is it against the law to do evil on the Sabbath or to do good? To destroy a life or to save one?" But no one answered him a word. ⁵Then looking around at everyone, Jesus was moved with*

indignation and grieved by the hardness of their hearts and said to the man, "Now stretch out your hand!" As he stretched out his hand, it was instantly healed! [6]After this happened, the Pharisees left abruptly and began to plot together with the friends and supporters of Herod Antipas on how they would kill Jesus. (Mark 3:1-6)

The message Jesus was committed to sharing (selling) was so controversial that from the early days of His ministry, those who ran the established religious system (His competition) sought to kill Him. Although the sales arena sometimes feels like a battleground, whatever we are selling doesn't carry the threat of death at the hand of our competitors. The fact that Jesus was willing to suffer even the consequence of death to deliver on His Word demonstrates how committed He was to fulfilling his mission.

What commitments are prudent for us to make and keep as it pertains to a sales relationship? The overarching commitment we've discussed is the dedication to reach mutually beneficial outcomes. We've also looked at various practical strategies to exhibit commitment such as: being a person of your word; showing yourself to be trustworthy; choosing to put others first; gaining a full understanding before presenting a solution; applying a diagnostic questioning process to help buyers come to their own conclusions; asking for a decision where a "yes" or a "no" is okay.

Another critical way to demonstrate commitment to the buyer is to take a long-term approach to relationship-building. That involves planning and implementing follow-up strategies to:

- keep in touch until a sale is made.
- check for satisfaction after the sale.
- ask for referrals.
- present new solutions to get added sales in the future.

Harvard Business Review stated, "Increasing customer retention by 5% boosts profits by 25%–90%."[13] In other words, cultivating relationships with customers ensures greater satisfaction and fosters additional sales. That customer retention process actually starts during the very first contact with the buyer, and it never stops.

Long-term Relationships vs. the One-call Close

Assigning value to long-term relationship building starts with the belief that it is beneficial. It begins with a conscious choice, and that choice then shapes our behavior. Face-to-face, phone, and even electronic sales all have a better chance to close when the salesperson (and company) chooses to operate with a mindset that values keeping in touch. Let's revisit the story of the roofing company salesman from the last chapter. What did his actions demonstrate? He asked no diagnostic questions, spoke from his script, collected yeses, and narrowed our options so we had to say "yes" so he could close immediately. He not only didn't try to build a relationship, his sales process violated basic human courtesies. It was obvious he had no intention of following up. He was in the "one-call close" business. "Buy now, or you're no use to me," is the impression he left on us.

Contrast that approach with making the effort to build lasting relationships by valuing people, respecting their right to say no, and wanting the best for them regardless of the outcome of the sales conversation. Here are two statistics on the benefits of doing follow-up that drive the point home:

- 80% of sales require 5 follow-up calls after the meeting. 44% of sales reps give up after 1 follow-up.[14]

---

[13] https://hbswk.hbs.edu/archive/the-economics-of-e-loyalty.

[14] https://blog.thebrevetgroup.com/21-mind-blowing-sales-stats.

- 80% of sales are made by 20% of salespeople.[15] The winners sell to the prospects the losers give up on.

Those who *do* follow up are positioned to reap the rewards of being consistently persistent.

Having a Follow-up Strategy is Critical

Follow-up takes time and discipline, but is worth doing for the success that implementing a follow-up system can bring. But persistence isn't enough. Having a single repository of customer data, where follow-up actions that you and others at your company perform are recorded, is essential. Customer Relationship Management (CRM) software is designed to help keep track of all the details pertaining to leads and customers. The various customer information data fields make it easy to "remember" important details and share information with others at the company who need to see it. The scheduling function, with automated reminders, minimizes the risk of overlooking important tasks. It doesn't matter what system you use; pick one and use it to its fullest capacity. A database is of no benefit unless it is used consistently.

Except for cold calls, your first sales contact with a buyer is actually a follow-up in which you respond to their inquiry asking for information. Without that callback, there is no sales opportunity. The timeliness of your response is also critical. The more time you let pass before you respond, the less likely you'll have a shot at the sale at all. The buyer contacted *you*. Your job is to follow up on her inquiry to engage her in the sales process as quickly as possible. Buyers don't give a second chance to a salesperson who doesn't respond in a timely fashion; they'll keep moving until they find someone who will.

---

[15] https://blog.hubspot.com/sales/80/20-rule-in-sales.

Consider ways that you can set up your next touch-point as you are finishing the conversation you're having. In essence, you close one conversation by setting expectations for what will happen next, which is the follow-up action you agree on together. Ask the buyer to tell you when you should follow up and what should happen next. Obtaining the buyer's help in shaping both when and what accomplishes two things: it helps the buyer to feel in control, and you are able to set clear expectations on action items and minimize potential misunderstandings. Here are a few examples of follow-up actions:

1. When an initial phone call results in an appointment being set, follow up immediately by sending a calendar invitation with names of all participants, location, time, and date. In a day or two, check to see that they have accepted the invitation. The day prior, call to confirm the meeting time and attendees. The day of, show up 5 minutes early.

2. When a sales meeting results in the need to create a proposal/quote/presentation, ask your prospect what he (and his colleagues) will want to see in the information presented. Get him, essentially, to write the outline for you, saving you guesswork that could result in providing information *you* think he needs but that he doesn't care about.

3. When a buyer doesn't give you her decision at the meeting and you have to follow up to get it, ask her when you should follow up, and get her to write your follow-up script. "I've made a note to call you on x date at x time. What exactly should I be asking you when we connect?" That question elicits more information about what needs to happen for her to be able to give you a decision.

4. When a buyer agrees to a follow-up timeframe and then seems to go into hiding mode and doesn't respond as agreed, say, "Mr. Prospect, I'm calling as we had agreed to see where you are in your decision-making process. I suspect it is taking longer than you anticipated due to circumstances beyond your control. That's okay. If you would be so kind

as to let me know how much of an extension you need, I will reset my follow-up call to you and get back to you then. Feel free to leave me a voicemail, text, or email with the new information."

5. When you've tried #4 and still received no response, say, "Mr. Prospect, I could be wrong, but I get the feeling something has changed. I want you to know that it's okay to tell me. I'd happily get back in touch with you at a later date, provide more details, or talk with your colleagues if any of those things would be helpful. I'd appreciate hearing back from you either way just so I don't keep bugging you with voicemails you'd rather not get. Thanks so much."

Your tone of voice in all cases needs to be friendly, non-judgmental, and helpful. The wrong tone used with even the perfect word choices will always come across badly.

Follow-up is Your Responsibility, Not the Buyer's

Buyers will say, "I'll get back to you." You've already realized that they typically don't. If you take them at their word, you're stuck in the awkward position of having to call and question them because they didn't follow through. You're most likely feeling a little resentful at having to make the call, and they probably won't answer because they know they've been remiss. You end up in voicemail. What message can you leave that will get them to call you back? You may *want* to say, "You were supposed to call me back with your answer by now. Why didn't you?" but you know you can't, so you try to soften it by saying, "Hi. I didn't hear back from you, so I wondered what decision you've made?" or something like that. And they still don't call you back.

It is so much easier to avoid all that discomfort by taking responsibility to own the follow-up process. When buyers say, "I'll get back to you," thank them and then explain what you prefer. Here are a couple examples: "I appreciate that. Now, I know you're a very busy person with lots of things that need your attention besides making a call back to me. If I don't hear from you at the appointed time, what would you have me do?" Or, "That would be great. Now, life has a way of throwing us curveballs, so on the outside chance that I don't hear from you, what would you have me do?" Buyers will typically give you permission to make a follow-up call to them when approached in this manner. Maintaining control of the follow-up process is the best way to keep the sales process moving forward while avoiding the awkwardness of guessing when to follow up and what to say.

Relationship Building Always Takes Two

It is important to realize that your best efforts to build lasting relationships are sometimes met with indifference. The choice to strive for long-term relationships, and to structure your interactions with others accordingly, is yours. Just remember that others may not value the same things you do. In the face of failed relationships, and even betrayals, it is possible to continue to demonstrate the willingness to keep building relationships by guarding your heart, and forgiving people when needed. It helps to remind yourself that they are not rejecting you. People always do things for their own reasons, not ours, and they don't always explain themselves. Jesus' opponents were many, yet He never rejected them as people, always remaining open to them having a change of heart. Taking a long-term relationship approach leaves the door open for future conversations that can bring value to both you and them.

Long-term Relationships and Teamwork

Sales are never made in complete isolation. By that I mean that, in addition to the salesperson, there are other people in various functional areas that are integral to the process of acquiring and servicing a customer. Marketing, customer service, billing, and delivery teams are among those that "touch" the buyer prior to, during, and/or after the sale is made. Jesus diligently sought and trained a team of people who could help Him follow through on His mission: [12]"After this, Jesus went up into the high hills to spend the whole night in prayer to God. [13]At daybreak he called together all of his followers and selected twelve from among them, and he appointed them to be his apostles." (Luke 6:12-13). You may not have a sales team that reports to you, but you can coordinate with others who also serve your customers.

It's important for you to be aware of the customer interface roles other team members play, and even consider taking the lead to elicit help from key employees so that the customer experience is the best it can possibly be. If you are a one-person company, there are vendors and freelancers you can hire to bring specialized assistance to the sales and follow-up processes. In the end, you own the customer relationship and are therefore the best person to educate and influence colleagues on how to serve your customer in the most effective way.

☞ Key Points to Remember:

1. A long-term relationship mindset will engender behaviors that build mutual respect, mutual trust, and mutual benefit.
2. Actions that are in keeping with a long-term relationship mindset include: being a person of your word; showing yourself to be trustworthy; choosing to put others first; gaining a full understanding before presenting a solution; applying a diagnostic questioning process to help buyers come to their own conclusions; asking for a decision where a "yes" or a "no" is okay; implementing a rigorous follow-up process to keep in touch with leads and customers.
3. Follow-up activities result in clear expectations being set about the next step in the sales process that are mutually agreed on.

4. Every relationship takes two. You can only do your part, and the other has the choice to reciprocate or not.
5. When you do your part to foster long-term relationships, most people respond positively, and you are able to have more productive conversations.
6. You own the follow-up process. Take the lead to coordinate with others who interact with the buyer to make sure the customer gets the best possible experience no matter what function is being performed.
7. Never reject a buyer; let her decide if she wants the relationship to continue or not.

() Action Steps:

1. Do you regularly follow up with prospects? If yes, continue here below. If no, go to #2.
   a. Make a list of all your follow-up activities.
   b. Evaluate the effectiveness of each activity.
   c. Identify any gaps in your follow-up process that came to light as you read this chapter.
   d. Create new follow-up actions to fill the gaps you identified.
   e. Practice using the new strategies.
2. If you don't have a follow up-system, why not...?
   a. What beliefs are you carrying that keep you from following up?
   b. What follow-up steps could you put in place that would have a high impact on your sales success quickly?
   c. How can you carve out the time needed to do follow-up activities?
3. What CRM (Customer Relationship Management) tool are you using today?
   a. If you don't have one, start researching CRMs now.
      i. Ask others in your industry which one they use and what they like about it.

    ii. Make a choice and implement it.

    iii. Be realistic with yourself about the learning curve you'll have to go through and find ways to grit your way through.

    iv. Use the CRM every day, all day, making notes immediately after a client interaction.

b. If you have a CRM, rate yourself on how well you are using it to keep track of customer interactions. Make a commitment to increase use of the tool. Hold yourself responsible to do it.

Chapter 9

The Law of the Harvest

⁷Make no mistake about it, God will never be mocked! For what you plant will always be the very thing you harvest. ⁸The harvest you reap reveals the seed that was planted. If you plant the corrupt seeds of self-life into this natural realm, you can expect to experience a harvest of corruption. If you plant the good seeds of Spirit-life you will reap the beautiful fruits that grow from the everlasting life of the Spirit. ⁹And don't allow yourselves to be weary or disheartened in planting good seeds, for the season of reaping the wonderful harvest you've planted is coming! (Galatians 6:7-9)

I live near Lancaster County, Pennsylvania, which holds the distinction of being the most productive non-irrigated farming

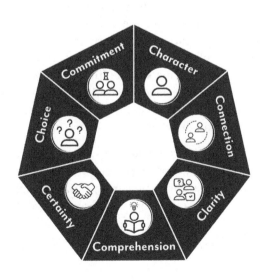

county in the United States.[16] Every year I relish watching a multitude of different crops as they progress through each stage of growth. From February through November, the fields transform from small green shoots to full-grown plants that flower and bear fruit. The harvest of each different crop delivers a special delight of fresh-picked tastes that can't be equaled by food that's been shipped in from far away.

The right seeds have to be planted at the right time in order to obtain the harvest that you want. Good seeds, good harvest. Bad seeds, bad harvest. But there is much more to successful farming than having good seed.

Farmers must prepare their fields prior to planting, and that preparation starts right after the harvest. Cover crops are often grown in order to naturally reintroduce nutrients that were drawn out of the soil by the previous crop. At the beginning of each growing season, the farmer plows and fertilizes to prepare the soil to receive the seed. They consider the weather for optimal timing of each planting. The fields must also be tended throughout the growing season: watered in times of drought, cultivated to deal with weeds, and watched for signs of pests that could destroy the crops. The harvest is timed according to plant maturity, and the crops properly stored for the farmer's use or sold for profit in a timely fashion so that the goods don't spoil. Preparation, sowing seed, cultivation, ingathering, and preparation again is the ongoing farming cycle. Skip any of the steps and there are negative consequences. It's the Law of the Harvest and it cannot be cheated.

Getting a good yield from your sales efforts follows a similar pattern of preparation, sowing seed, cultivation, and ingathering, which circle back again to preparing. Take the right actions, in the right sequence, timing, and frequency, and the cycle

---

[16] https://co.lancaster.pa.us/DocumentCenter/View/139/Lancaster-County-Farming-Facts-5th-edition.

continues, resulting in new and repeat sales. Just like the farmer, salespeople can't skip any of the steps, do them out of sequence, or "hope and wish" for the harvest to occur. The work must be done or there will be no yield.

Each of the seven characteristics of Jesus that we've examined is comprised of specific actions that contribute to ethical sales practices that make it possible to reap a bountiful harvest in due season. Character, connection, clarity, comprehension, certainty, choice, and commitment each in themselves involve intentionality on your part. It requires inner strength, discipline, and determination to implement these strategies consistently in a world where shortcuts are a constant temptation.

How to Stay the Course and Reap the Harvest

If you've read this far, it is because you are serious about living your values in the marketplace, and because you are no longer content with things as they've always been. You believe there is a better way. You can be the better way when you make a conscious decision to integrate what you've learned, what you believe, and what you value into your sales process. It is much easier to speak and act out of habit, blindly relying on chance to carry you through. Any alternative to that auto-pilot behavior takes a conscious and determined effort. In my experience, few people are willing to do what it takes to reap the rewards that only transpire as a result of committing to diligently implementing the strategies that I have shared. Only by integrating what you've learned into your everyday life will change occur. I recommend three ways to help you stay the course: pray, practice, and teach.

First, pray.

"But Jesus often slipped away from them and went into the wilderness to pray" (Luke 5:16). Jesus prayed to gain wisdom from God, and so can we. Ask the Lord to help you make the changes you want to make. Ask him for innovative, creative strategies that you can implement as you sell. Ask for His wisdom in the moment, even in the middle of a conversation when you don't know what to say next. Seek the Lord for advice and He will answer.

Second, practice, knowing that as you change, others may react in unexpected ways.

[12]*After this* ("this" refers to the Wedding at Cana where Jesus did His first miracle of turning water into wine)[17], *Jesus, his mother and brothers and his disciples went to Capernaum and stayed there for a few days.* [13]*But the time was close for the Jewish Passover to begin, so Jesus walked to Jerusalem.* [14]*As he went into the temple courtyard, he noticed it was filled with merchants selling oxen, lambs, and doves for exorbitant prices, while others were overcharging as they exchanged currency behind their counters.* [15]*So Jesus found some rope and made it into a whip. Then he drove out every one of them and their animals from the courtyard of the temple, and he kicked over their tables filled with money, scattering it everywhere!* [16]*And he shouted at the merchants, "Get these things out of here! Don't you dare make my Father's house into a center for merchandise!"*

(John 2:12-16)

Of the three Gospel writers that mention the upending of the merchant's tables in the Temple area (Matthew 21:12; Mark 11:15; John 2:15), John is the only one who mentions it in the context of the first days of Jesus' ministry. I find this significant because it indicates that early in His ministry, not just at the Passover prior to His death and resurrection, Jesus "turned the tables" on the established merchant practices of the day, stirring

---

[17] Author's addition in parentheses.

up enmity from those who benefited from the marketing and sales "status quo."

Why is this significant? Because when you start to reap the benefit from the new approach you're taking with buyers, it may cause colleagues and friends to become envious of your new-found success. Whenever we make changes in ourselves, there is a ripple effect on those around us because change brings with it a level of unpredictability. When it happens, don't be surprised. Evaluate the source and respond accordingly. With colleagues and loved ones that we need to continue to get along with, explain where you're coming from. With competitors, take it as a compliment and keep doing what you're doing!

Some modern-day examples of upsetting the tables (the status quo) include:

1. If you are in an industry that requires a bid process to win business, you are leveraging every possibility to engage in dialogue in addition to submitting the obligatory bid forms.
2. If you are in a "non-selling" profession (doctor, lawyer, engineer, accountant, etc.), you are proactively engaging in sales activities in calculated ways that are in keeping with your personal and professional ethics.
3. When you don't know something, you don't hesitate to admit it. Then you do research and get back to the buyer with an answer.
4. You have a tight focus on who your ideal client is and you stick to it.
5. When you can't do what is being asked, and you know it is not good for your business to try, you refer the work to a company that specializes in what the buyer needs.

Third, teach others what you've learned.

One of the best ways to ensure our own learning is to teach someone else. Although the focus of this book has been the sales conversation, the strategies put forth will work when applied to any conversation, with anyone. Some of the greatest victories my clients have shared are about restored relationships, deeper conversations, and greater understanding with their family members. Teenagers respond particularly well, and provide a great place to practice your new approach. Teaching them how to do what you're doing will help equip them for greater success at work and in life, too.

It is my sincere desire that this book has encouraged you to live your faith with courage and boldness that transforms every conversation you have. I'll conclude by praying this prayer from Colossians 1:9-11 over you:

...[I keep] you always in [my] prayers that you would receive the perfect knowledge of God's pleasure over your [life], making you [a reservoir] of every kind of wisdom and spiritual understanding. [I] pray that you would walk in the ways of true righteousness, pleasing God in every good thing you do. Then you'll become [a fruit-bearing branch], yielding to his life and maturing in the rich experience of knowing God in his fullness! And [I] pray that you would be energized with all his explosive power from the realm of his magnificent glory, filling you with great hope.[18]

You can pray this *same* prayer over yourself, too:

Lord, I ask you bless me and make me a reservoir of your wisdom and spiritual understanding. Help me walk in the ways of true righteousness, pleasing you in everything that I do—at work and at home, with colleagues, with friends, and with family. Help me be a fruitful branch yielded to your will in my life so I can experience and know you fully. Energize my efforts with the explosive power that is born from your Glory, and fill me with great hope for all the things you will do through me as I yield my efforts to your will. In Jesus' mighty name, Amen.

---

[18] Modified by the author to read in the first person.

❧ Key Points to Remember:

1. The Law of the Harvest is immutable; it can't be cheated.

2. Change occurs when we put what we know into action. Jesus said, [24]"Everyone who hears my teaching and applies it to his life can be compared to a wise man who built his house on an unshakable foundation. [25]When the rains fell and the flood came, with fierce winds beating upon his house, it stood firm because of its strong foundation." (Matthew 7:24-25).

3. Pray, practice, and teach others to do what you've learned to advance your skills quickly.

◖◗ Action Steps:

1. How has your opinion about sales changed from before reading this book until now?

2. What is your plan to implement what you've learned?

3. Pick one specific behavior that you can start with.
   a. Track how often you do that behavior, along with comments about how it worked. If results aren't what you wanted, make adjustments and try again.
   b. Be realistic about anything that might get in the way of your success and have a plan to overcome it.
   c. Remind yourself of the benefits you will reap as a reward for doing the hard work to implement your new strategies.
   d. Start immediately.
   e. Celebrate your successes as they occur.

4. What preconceived ideas did you have about sales and how have those ideas changed?

5. With whom can you share what you've learned?

Appendix 1
Sales Process

The following steps can be adapted to any type of sales—tangibles, intangibles, products, services, phone, in person—for any type of business or industry. Obviously, how you execute each step will be based on your unique position in the marketplace. This represents a sales process flow. The content and context of your conversations will be unique to your business focus. In its shortest form, effective sales processes include these six steps:

- Prepare
- Set expectations
- Qualify
    - Pain
    - Budget
    - Decision process
- Close
- Present, Deliver, Follow through
- Evaluate

See below for more detail on the process.

Preparation/Marketing

Clearly identify your ideal customer characteristics.

Develop a sales plan to reach your ideal buyers.

Schedule sales activities on the calendar to reach new leads and keep in touch with existing leads that are not ready to buy yet.

Preparation/Sales

Research your leads to learn as much about their company, industry, challenges, and potential reasons why they might buy from you.

Set up phone or face-to-face sales meetings on your calendar. Explain approximately how much time you'll need, and set expectations about what will be discussed.

Prepare a list of questions you want to ask to get a deeper understanding of the person/company you are to meet with.

Confirm the appointment.

On the Sales Call

Set Expectations

Verbally set expectations with the prospect so that both of you know and agree on what will be discussed during the sales call. Set the stage for the potential outcomes: Yes, move forward to the next step; or, No, don't move forward because there isn't a good fit.

Qualify

Ask questions to discover if the prospect has:

1. A problem you can solve (pain).
2. The resources to pay for your product/service (budget).
3. The ability to make the decision to move forward with the purchase (decision).

Determine Next Steps

Depending on the outcome of the qualifying steps, you may either:

1. Decide not to do business together.
2. Close the sale and set expectations about what will happen next.
3. Post-sales call follow-up and follow-through

If the meeting did not result in a sale, gather information about why not so you can learn from it.

If the meeting resulted in a sale, set expectations for delivery and communicate your ongoing customer care promises.

As much as we would like it, many initial contacts do not end in a definitive yes or no. For these it is important to have a system to keep in touch so that the lead is nurtured until such time that the prospect makes a decision one way or the other.

Appendix 2

Prayer of Salvation/ Rededication

If you have never given your life to Jesus, it's easy. Say this prayer out loud, from your heart and you'll find new life in Him.

Father God in heaven, I believe that you love me so much that you sent your Son, Jesus Christ, to earth to be born of a virgin, to live a holy life, and to die on the cross to pay the ultimate price for my sins. I believe that you raised Jesus from the dead to prove He is the only way of salvation. I believe the blood of Jesus was poured out to cleanse me of my sins. Father God, I ask you to forgive me for my sins and wash them away with the blood of Jesus. Lord Jesus, I ask you to come into my heart and be my Lord and Savior. I trust you alone for my salvation. Thank you for all that you have done and will do for me. Amen.

Appendix 3

Prayer to Dedicate Your Business to God

God's promises for your business can be found in Deuteronomy 8:18, 28:1-6, 29:9, Psalms 1:1-3, and Proverbs 3:3-10. If you have not yet dedicated your business or your work-efforts to the Lord, this prayer can serve as a guide to doing so.

Father God, in the name of your Son, Jesus Christ, I dedicate my business/work/career to you. You are my C.E.O. and I want to please you in all my business activities. Bless every conversation I have and every decision that I make so that my actions reflect Your Glory at work, just as it is in Heaven. Holy Spirit, I ask you to guide me and give me wisdom in the moment so that I always do what is right, and say what is pleasing to God. Thank you that I am not alone, for you promise to be with me in all things, including the work that I do. Thank you for prosperity, provision and blessing that are mine because I follow your ways and have submitted all my work-efforts to you. In Jesus Name I pray, amen.

Other Products and Services

If you are interested in learning how to develop your sales skills to get more results for yourself and/or your team, Deb can help. For more information about any of the following services, contact Deb Brown Sales at this email address: deb@debbrownsales.com.

Executive Coaching for business owners and key leaders.

One-on-one and team sales coaching.

Keynote speaking, workshops, and trainings at corporate and non-profit meetings, conferences, and retreats.

For individual learning opportunities, Deb teaches regularly online. You can request to join the private "Sell Like Jesus" Facebook group where you can connect with a community of others on the same journey as you. More training and workshop opportunities will be announced there: https://www.facebook.com/groups/SellLikeJesus/.

Get a free, downloadable PDF of the "Sell Like Jesus Workbook" which contains all chapter summaries and action steps by going to: www.debbrownsales.com/sljworkbook.

Visit www.debbrownsales.com/resources for blog posts with additional sales tips.

For more information about Christian sales leadership strategies, please contact us at deb@debbrownsales.com.

About the Author

Deborah Brown Maher, the President and Founder of Deb Brown Sales and author of the Sell Like Jesus® blog, is known for getting sales teams results that are congruent with individuals' and companies' core values. Her professional background spans over thirty years of solid expertise in all levels of sales execution, demonstrated by a consistently successful track record in both business-to-business and business-to-consumer sales across a wide range of industries and businesses of every size—small, medium, or large—from start-up to multi-national. What makes Deb unique in the coaching world is her real-life sales experience coupled with her ability to successfully transfer her knowledge and skills to others through one-on-one and group coaching. She is particularly recognized for helping her clients get and sustain the bottom-line results they are seeking.

As sole proprietor of DLBRB, Inc. in the 1990's, Deb was engaged by a variety of well-known companies such as AMP, Incorporated, Hershey Foods, and AT&T/Avaya, where she helped the Harrisburg business-to-business sales office improve their sales ranking from 61st to #1 out of 62 offices in their business unit in just eighteen months.

Deb put her own practice aside to join a unique entrepreneurial team at a Carlisle, PA-based technology start-up called PestPatrol. As Vice President of Sales, she spearheaded the business-to-business sales unit, growing revenues from zero to $8 million in 3 years, whereupon the company was acquired by Computer Associates, Inc. (CA, Inc.). Deb continued at CA in a Product Champion role, responsible for global sales of "threat management products," from 2004-2006, growing sales to over $21 million. During that time she played a pivotal liaison role between various departments, assuring that the needs of the end-users were being translated into new iterations of the products. She also trained business-to-business sales teams in the USA, EMEA, and Asia to facilitate sales growth world-wide.

More recently, as President of Deb Brown Sales, Deb has been working with business owners and their sales and service teams in Central Pennsylvania and nationally. Her market sector experience is extensive, including Construction, Communications, Consultancy, Dentistry, Energy, Education, Financial, Fine Arts, Insurance, Legal, Marketing/Advertising/ Media, Manufacturing, Medical, Non-Profit & Faith Based, Publishing, Commercial and Residential Real Estate, Retail, Start-up Companies, Telecommunications, and Technology.

Deb was also instrumental in helping a London-based company, Prosell, Ltd., secure an account with Comcast Cable to provide leadership training and coaching to enhance sales and customer service performance. Together with the Prosell team, she developed a customized program to meet the unique needs of this Fortune 500 company. The work she and the Prosell team did is credited with increasing bottom line profits by $2.8 billion during the first 8-month period after the program launched in 2010. Their successful work continues to the present (2019).

A *cum laude* graduate of Allegheny College, Meadville PA, Deb earned a B.A. in Latin American Studies. She is a voracious reader who values life-long learning and loves keeping up with the newest research in sales psychology, sociology, quantum physics, how the brain works, and effective communication strategies—all of which find their way into her ever-evolving training and coaching programs.

In her leisure time, Deb is an accomplished and acclaimed fine-artist, primarily in acrylics and watercolors, whose work is sold through Art & Soul Gallery, Camp Hill, PA and online at Worshipful Art. Since 1998 she has been a frequent featured speaker and painter at national and international non-profit conferences. Bi-lingual, she is fluent in Spanish, both written and spoken.

Deb is married to Charles Maher, a retired Senior Master Sergeant in the United States Air Force. Active members of a local church, they both freely volunteer their time to minister to others, praying for anyone in need of mental, physical or emotional healing. Deb and Charles both love cats, and currently dote on one Ragdoll named Queen Sheba Hailey. Deb also has a tremendous green thumb, proudly growing enough organic vegetables for personal consumption and to share with friends.

Deb Brown Maher

Visit us online at:

www.debbrownsales.com

facebook.com/SellLikeJesus/

Made in the USA
Middletown, DE
23 December 2019